"A classic of theological vignettes. Sharply profiles thinkers on a new frontier. Scuttles the myth that liberation theologies are a system."

Frederick Herzog
Duke University

"It is particularly important to know the contexts out of which theology is being created. These 36 portraits will help us understand the questions to which liberation theologians are attempting to respond so that we can understand their thought and their actions more accurately. There is an added benefit: not only will we know them better, but the process through which they go can help us to understand ourselves better as well."

Robert McAfee Brown
Professor Emeritus, Pacific School of Religion

Deane William Ferm

PROFILES
IN
LIBERATION

36 Portraits of Third World Theologians

TWENTY-THIRD PUBLICATIONS

Mystic, Connecticut

Twenty-Third Publications
185 Willow Street
P.O. Box 180
Mystic CT 06355
(203) 536-2611

ISBN 0-89622-377-9
Library of Congress Catalog Card Number 88-72013

To the Memory of
My Daughter Laurie
(1956-1985)

A Sisseton Sioux
and
Her Struggle for Liberation

Acknowledgments

I want to thank every theologian featured in this book. They themselves are the inspiration for this volume; for their generous responses and their crucial work, I am deeply grateful. I only hope that I have done justice to each one of them. I also wish to thank Robert R. Barr for his fine translation assistance with the questionnaires.

But I must single out two individuals without whose patience and encouragement I would never have finished the first paragraph. First, my editor, Stephen Scharper of Twenty-Third Publications. How can an editor be so gentle, yet so darned persuasive? Thanks, Stephen. Second, I thank my co-author Debra who is also my wife, my lover, my teacher, my best friend, and severest critic. I simply could not have done it without her.

CONTENTS

Profiles in Liberation
36 Portraits of Third World Theologians

INTRODUCTION

Third World liberation theology has been my major scholarly interest over the past several years. It dates back to the spring of 1983 when—like a bolt out of the blue—Philip Scharper, founding editor of Orbis Books, telephoned and asked me to write a book surveying Third World liberation theology. The results of that phone call were *Third World Liberation Theologies: An Introductory Survey,* and *A Reader* (Orbis Books, 1986).

The longer I study this subject, the more I come to realize that there is no such thing as a single, codified *Third World Liberation Theology.* Indeed, there is as much variety and complexity to be found in Third World liberation theology today as there is in theology itself. Who today would even dare to try to define the term "theology" in a way that would be acceptable to all theologians? Similar difficulties would befall anyone attempting to define "liberation" theology in such a manner. We must, therefore, for the sake of accuracy, speak of Third World *theologies.*

Take the term *liberation. Liberation from what?* Many critics of Third World liberation theology reduce the meaning of the *liberation* to its political-socio-economic dimension. Quite obviously this dimension of liberation is important to all liberation theologies found throughout the Third World. Indeed I know of no Third World liberation theologian from Africa, Asia or Latin America who ignores this dimension or, equally important, confines the meaning of liberation to this dimension alone. To say, therefore, that it is the *only* aspect of liberation is to misinterpret liberation theology.

Further, the basic point on which all Third World liberation theologians agree is that liberation theology has its roots in spiritual experience, i.e., in a committed faith in God and Jesus Christ. Now, to be sure, in some areas, such as Latin America, South Africa and South Korea, the political-socio-economic dimension of liberation looms larger than in other regions. Consider the debate raging among African theologians as to which should take priority: political-socio-economic liberation or *cultural* liberation (i.e., the desire on the part of Africans Christians to reflect their own heritage and not the Western imports.) Manas Buthelezi of South Africa, for example, emphasizes the priority of political-socio-

1

economic liberation to such an extent that he considers cultural liberation a ploy, an effort to deflect attention from the nitty-gritty socio-econimic issues. On the other hand, John Mbiti of Kenya objects so strongly to Buthelezi's view that he himself rejects the label "liberation" theologian. Still other African liberation theologians, such as Zambian Emmanuel Milingo, stress the healing process as the primary form of liberation. Then, too, in the vast continent of Asia where Christians are a tiny minority, liberation from Christian provincialism becomes so central that some Asian liberation theologians have replaced the Latin American notion of *Christian* base communities with the expanded concept of *human* base communities. Liberation does indeed take many different forms throughout the Third World.

One feature of Third World liberation theologies can be applied universally, however: All liberation theologies seek to be indigenous to their own particular historical contexts and emerge from small base Christian (or human) communities of the poor and oppressed who, through the continuing process of action and reflection on their spiritual and biblical roots (*praxis*), develop their own theology in tune with their own hopes and fears. They are theologies which begin "from below," theologies of "ascent" rather than "descent," as Leonardo Boff and others have succinctly put it. Indigenization is the key component of all Third World liberation theologies. (For this reason I have included John Mbiti despite his very legitimate misgivings about the term "liberation.") Placing the emphasis on indigenization makes matters even more complex! The water buffaloes of Kosuke Koyama's missionary experience in Thailand simply do not mesh with the mestizo culture of Gustavo Gutiérrez's Peru or the vicious apartheid system of Desmond Tutu's South Africa.

I make no secret of my contention that one of my major reasons for writing this book is to dismantle once and for all the arguments of those critics who insist that Third World liberation theology can be confined to one monolithic system. To achieve this objective I have selected 36 Third World liberation theologians from Africa, Asia, and Latin America. (Because of space constraints I have had to eliminate several equally important individuals.) I have read most of their writings that have been translated into English. Even more important, during the years 1987 and 1988 I have corresponded with them and sent them questionnaires that asked their views on a variety of issues, including their understanding of liberation theology, how their views and the issues have changed over the past ten years, and the role of Marxist analysis in their theology. I also asked them to tell their own personal stories to explain how they arrived at their theological views, including the crucial events that had shaped their lives. The correspondence and questionnaires constitute the raw materials for this book, and, unless otherwise indicated, quotations of the theologians are taken from these sources. I wanted to hear directly from these individuals what *they* believe and not—as is usually the case—what we *think* they believe.

From their letters, questionnaires and other writings I have drawn up a profile of each theologian which outlines his or her background, theological development and distinctive contributions to date. Although I have tried my best to be both fair and accurate, I have obviously given my own interpretation and take full responsibility if I have erred in any respects. I have also included a brief select bibliography for each indivdual.

I must confess, however, to one grave disappointment and that is that I have not included more women theologians. I have tried, but the vagaries of postal services have frustrated my efforts. I sincerely hope that others will meet with better success than I in giving more female Third World liberation theologians the critical attention they deserve.

Common Responses

Three of the questions I raised in my questionnaire received such similar replies that I have decided to summarize these responses in this Introduction. First, I asked: "How do the issues that you confront in the Third World today differ from a decade ago?" The virtually *unanimous* response was that the political and socio-economic problems are more urgent, pressing, and complex today. In a nutshell: The poor are becoming poorer, and the rich are becoming richer. This fact is primarily attributable, as Engelbert Mveng suggests, to the "growing imbalance between the First and the Third World." As Kofi Appiah-Kubi comments: "The focus has become sharper and more urgent.... These challenges do not end." In addition, many theologians agree with the observation of José Comblin that there is "more consciousness of the diversity of problems in the Third World." Mercy Amba Oduyoye, for example, observes that a decade ago "there was an initial emphasis on political-economic analysis which tended to put a muzzle on other factors, e.g., feminist perspectives." Otto Maduro notes that, unlike ten years ago, Third World liberation theologians have become more sensitive to the oppression of women, the destruction of the natural environment and the possibility of a nuclear holocaust. The responses clearly indicate that Third World liberation theologians have in recent years come to realize that liberation encompasses a great many more dimensions than previously thought. In this sense, it is abundantly evident that Third World liberation theology is an ever-changing and growing phenomenon that seeks to read and respond to the "signs of the times."

A second question that received a similarly uniform response was: "What do you consider to be the major misperceptions that critics have of Third World liberation theology." The responses can be divided into three closely related categories. First—and unanimously—Third World liberation theology is *not* a child of Marxist ideology. To be sure, these theologians do differ in their utilization of Marxist analysis; their responses range from José Comblin's remark that "Marxism is unavoidable in the Third World....There is no alternative" to Segundo Galilea's contention that "I was never attracted by Marxist analysis." The point I want to underscore here is that every theologian contacted objected vociferously to the contention of some critics that Third World liberation theology is, in Leonardo Boff's apt phrase, "simply a Trojan horse by which Marxism infiltrates society and gets the poor, who are religious, to revolt." As Aloysius Pieris suggests, there is a "false understanding (on the part of church leaders) of liberation theology as a Marxist wolf clothed in a sheep's skin." Most of these theologians would agree with Ernesto Cardenal's comment that "Marxism plays in our theology the role Aristotelianism had in that of Saint Thomas Aquinas." I am also convinced that all of these theologians would concur with Desmond Tutu that "any ideology that denies that men and women are created in the image of God is incompatible with Christianity."

Another misperception cited by these theologians—with *unanimity and frustration*—is one to which I have already referred: the identification of liberation exclusively with a political-socio-economic understanding. Míguez Bonino laments the fact that "once people have decided that liberation theology is 'only' political liberation, all other expressions are read as marginal, secondary or even disguises." These theologians would agree completely with Otto Maduro that liberation theology is "a spiritual, religious theology in its own right." In short: *The spiritual-theological-transcendent-biblical-prayerful* component is primary and absolutely indispensable.

A final error is the tendency of many to equate Third World liberation theology with Latin American liberation theology. In the first place, Latin American liberation theology is by no means monolithic; and, in the second place, as Samuel Rayan emphasizes, it is just plain inaccurate to contend that "there is only one type of liberation theology, the one that originated in Latin America, and that the Asian and African liberation theologies are borrowing from Latin America." Asian and African forms of liberation theology are indigenous. But even more to the point is the fact that Third World liberation theologians strongly believe that liberation theology contains a message for all Christians. Enrique Dussel argues that it is wrong to believe that liberation theology is "of Latin America alone (instead of the world) and principally valid for the Marxist Third World." José Miranda puts the matter even more bluntly: "We raise a universal issue. At stake is the essence of Christianity." Here Tissa Balasuriya's concept of a *planetary* theology is crucial.

The global implications of liberation theologies relate to a third question put to the theologians. Because this book was envisioned primarily for a North American readership, I asked: "What impact would you hope that your theology would have on North America?" Here the responses consistently underscored two points. First: *Please heed the cries of the poor and oppressed throughout the Third World.* What Samuel Rayan writes could have come from all 36 theologians: "I wish my work could help people to appreciate the struggles of the poor the world over, and recognize the active presence of God for our day." The crucial phrase here is the struggles of the poor and oppressed *the world over.* And here these Third World theologians challenge the citizens of the United States to become more aware of the evil deeds perpetrated by the *excesses* of capitalism—when the profit motive becomes so much more important than the humanitarian motive. Pablo Richard asks North Americans to focus their attention upon "the *North-South contradiction*—the contradiction between the *poor peoples* of the world, the *poor* of all peoples, and the *power centers* which are in the developed world." He insists: "Our enemy is *not* communism, but poverty and oppression." Tissa Balasuriya speaks for his colleagues when he expresses the hope that "the United States trust more in God than in the dollar, that U.S. churches be more genuinely Christian and combat the evil of capitalism as it exists from within its metropolis." The words of Aloysius Pieris should be taken to heart: "America—like the church as a whole—is too involved in fighting Marxism, instead of eliminating injustice and exploitation.... If, by a miracle, America opts for elimination of unjust structures, beginning with domestic structures, Marxism would become irrelevant."

Mercy Amba Oduyoye's conviction that *Third World* liberation theology in reality refers to "all who do theology from the context of injustice and unrighteousness" intimates that North Americans should themselves become "Third World" theologians in confronting their own bailiwick, their own indigenous injustice and unrighteousness. Let's face it. In the United States of America the gap between the rich and the poor, between blacks and whites, is also becoming greater. And what about the plight of the blacks, the native Americans, the Chicanos, the homeless, the unemployed, the handicapped, and all North American poor who suffer from injustice and unrighteousness? We can't sweep their poverty under the table. José Miranda is on target when he affirms: "I would like to bring to North America a conception of Christianity more in accordance with what Jesus taught and did.... The future of the human race, as far as we can now see, depends on North America."

Finally, if I were to pick out one phrase that I dream would be the response to this book, it would be a phrase that Philip Scharper often used: "mission in reverse." Gone are the days when mission was a one-way street from the First World to the Third World. Now is the time for "mission in reverse": from the Third World to the First World, from the exploited to the oppressor, from the poor to the complacent. I sincerely hope that this book will be a catalyst in this process.

PART I

AFRICA

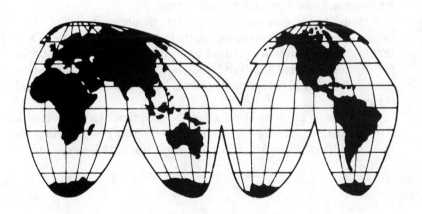

Liberation theology on the continent of Africa has emerged primarily as a response to white oppression and western imperialism. A critical component of African liberation theology is *cultural* liberation. Indeed this emphasis on indigenization is so strong that many African theologians argue that African black theology, with its stress on socio-economic-political oppression, and African theology, with its over-riding concern for cultural issues, should be considered separately.

I reject this view. I agree with Desmond Tutu that these two approaches should be considered soul mates and not antagonists. Despite their obvious differences, Tutu insists: "I see remarkable similarities between African theology and Black theology and I contend that they have a great deal to learn from one another and to give to each other." (*Black Theology: A Documentary History, 1966-1979.* Edited by Gayraud S. Wilmore and James H. Cone. Maryknoll, N.Y.: Orbis Books, 1979, p. 489). Of course, an obvious reason for the different emphases is the divergent historical contexts: black theology emerging primarily in South Africa with its vicious white racism, and African theology emanating from those African countries now under black control.

A third factor endemic to liberation theology in Africa is the importance some theologians attach to the gift of healing. These theologians insist that spiritual healing must be the foundation for authentic liberation—and that both the cultural and socio-economic-political components should be by-products of this healing process.

To illustrate all three approaches to liberation I have selected 12 African theologians. The diversity of their profiles indicates that liberation theology in Africa is a many-splendored phenomenon.

KOFI APPIAH-KUBI

If the churches in Africa are to grow and develop, they must be allowed to take root in the soil of Africa where they have been planted. In this Africanization process the Indigenous African churches have made a break-through and have a great deal to teach the missionary churches (Indigenous African Christian Churches: Signs of Authenticity, *p. 122).*

9

Kofi Appiah-Kubi is a firm advocate of the indigenization of Christianity in its African cultural setting. In making indigenization his primary focus he believes that spiritual hunger as seen in "healing, divining, prophesying, and visioning" is more important to the African people than "political, social, economic, and racial factors" (p. 118).

Appiah-Kubi was born in the small town of Nkawkaw in the eastern region of Ghana in 1934. As a youngster he attended Presbyterian mission schools. During these years the Christian missionaries did not permit the Ghanians to use their own Ghanian names. Instead the Ghanians were given Christian, i.e., Western names. Nor were national costumes—not even the national Kente Cloth—permitted. Appiah-Kubi recalls that a major turning point in his life occurred the day that an acting Ghanian principal allowed the students to wear their own Kente Cloth—even to church! "We went to church for the first time all clad in our Kente Cloth expecting the worst to happen. But thank God the chapel did not collapse on our heads!" Appiah-Kubi goes on to say: "This revealed to me that God does not want to turn us Ghanians into Europeans and Americans before we can serve and worship. This was a turning point in my life....I started to study the customs, culture and language of my people."

Appiah-Kubi traveled to England for his undergraduate work, receiving a B.A. from the University of Hull in sociology and theology in 1970 and a B.Litt. from Oxford in social anthropology in 1973. He did his graduate work at Columbia University, earning a master's degree and finally a doctorate in public health in 1982. He has served as teacher and headmaster at various secondary schools in Ghana and since 1983 has been a research associate at the Olive W. Garvey Center for the Improvement of Human Functioning in Tema, Ghana. He has also been a member of the board of directors of the Ecumenical Institute in Geneva.

As a Presbyterian lay theologian, Appiah-Kubi has concentrated his efforts on meshing African cultural values with the understanding, development, and growth of Christianity on the African continent. But by no means does he neglect the imperative to liberate Africa's political, social, economic, and racial victims. He does believe, however, that such liberation can best be achieved through the process of cultural liberation. It is in the dimension of cultural liberation that the Euro-American missionary churches have failed so completely, a failure that has led to the tremendous growth of the independent churches. Appiah-Kubi maintains that African forms of worship, ministry, and music must be in harmony with African lives and needs. In this process of indigenization, Christians should at the same time expand their vision of God at work in all cultures. Appiah-Kubi writes: "I reject the traditional affirmation that Christianity alone holds the absolute truth. By so doing, Western evangelists have arrogated unto themselves the sense of having the truth, and of having the pure culture and therefore the true religion, to near denial of any moral, ethical, or religious values of African religion" ("Response," p. 128).

Two distinctive characteristics of African native religions are the importance of healing and reverence for ancestors. In his book *Man Cures, God Heals: Religion and Medical Practice among the Akans of Ghana* Appiah-Kubi explains the cardinal importance of the healing process for his people. They consider disease to be a state of bodily disharmony. They make no distinction between religion and medicine nor between religion and culture. Moreover, for the Akans, their ancestors are the custodians of morality. Through direct communication with these ancestors the Akan faith-healers claim that they are drawing directly upon the same spiritual resources as Jesus himself did in restoring the sick to health. Neglect of these African understandings is another reason why the missionary churches have lost membership to the independent churches. Appiah-Kubi notes: "Ancestor veneration is totally neglected by the mission churches, while at the same time they urge their members to worship a Saint George of England, a Saint Andrew of Scotland, or a Saint Christopher of the Vatican" (p. 87).

Appiah-Kubi is careful to point out that Jesus Christ remains the focal point of the indigenous Christian churches. "He is the Savior, the Baptizer in the Spirit, the Soon-Coming-King, and the Healer" ("Indigenous African Christian Churches: Signs of Authenticity," p. 118). Likewise the Bible remains central to the lives of the members of these churches. In fact, these people read the Bible so much that they have been nicknamed "the people with the dirty Bible." For them the Bible is a living record of how the voice of God can be heard through human beings who are filled with the Holy Spirit, in particular, the "priest-healers" who encourage their people to express their feelings through clapping, dancing, and the beating of drums. Appiah-Kubi underscores the importance of feeding the spiritual hunger of these people as a means to political, social, and economic liberation.

Appiah-Kubi also points out that the indigenous churches have incorporated many other features of native African religions, such as festivals. One of the most important for the Akans is the naming ceremony which usually takes place the seventh or eighth day after a baby's birth. By tradition each child is given the name that corresponds with the day of the week: Kofi for a Friday-born male, Akosua for a Sunday-born female, and so on. Another important ceremony is marriage, for which the banana plant, which grows in such large numbers in Kenya, is the fertility symbol. Then, too, following native practice, the indigenous churches have whole-heartedly welcomed women as church leaders and prophets.

Marxism as an ideology has had no discernible impact on Appiah-Kubi's thinking. To be sure, if Marxism means "from each according to his or her ability, to each according to his or her needs," then obviously Marxism makes sense in the African world, which teems with social inequalities, greed, and waste. But what is distinctively Marxist about the above statement? Surely it comes out of the Christian message! Appiah-Kubi acknowledges that "to the misinformed and the uninformed, liberation theologians are a bunch of communists! We are painfully accused of being Marxists." So Appiah-Kubi, as with all Third World liberation theologians, is adamant that his urgent concern for human justice and need, for a more equitable sharing of the earth's resources, comes straight from his biblical faith.

For Appiah-Kubi, then, cultural and linguistic liberation are important pillars for the propagation of the Christian faith on the African continent. Echoing the ancient psalmist, he asks: How can I sing the Lord's song in a strange land and language? (Psalm 137). A careful reading of the gospels reveals a healing Jesus, an image that has been sorely neglected in many Western versions of Christianity. It is this ministry of healing that should receive the importance it deserves. Indeed, it is through the healing process that full-fledged liberation begins. "Jesus said: 'I have come that ye may have life and have it more abundantly.' But my constant question is: where is this abundant life amidst poverty, hunger, disease, want and impoverishment?" Appiah-Kubi believes that his basic challenge as a liberation theologian is the same as that of the prophet Jeremiah: "Is there no balm in Gilead? Is there no physician there? Why then has the health of the daughter of my people not been restored?" (Jeremiah 8:22).

BOOKS

Psychology, Religion and Healing: A Sociological Survey of Healing Practices among the Akans of Ghana. Kumasi, Ghana: University Press, U.S.T., 1979.

African Theology En Route. Edited by Kofi Appiah-Kubi and Sergio Torres. Maryknoll, N.Y. : Orbis Books, 1979.

Man Cures, God Heals: Religion and Medical Practice among the Akans of Ghana. Totowa, N.J.: Allanheld Press, Osman and Co., 1981.

ARTICLES

"The Church's Healing Ministry in Africa," *Contact*, No. 29. Geneva: Christian Medical Commission, World Council of Churches, 1975.

"Indigenous African Christian Churches: Signs of Authenticity," *African Theology En Route*, pp. 117-126.

"Response," *Christ's Lordship and Religious Pluralism*. Edited by Gerald H. Anderson and Thomas F. Stransky. Maryknoll, N.Y.: Orbis Books, 1981, pp. 120-129.

ALLAN BOESAK

Christian faith transcends all ideologies and all national-istic ideals. It transcends specific groups and nations with their special ideals and interests. That is to say, to have political ideals is not in itself sinful; to identify them with the gospel of Jesus Christ is (Farewell to Innocence, p. 121).

In the country of South Africa, wracked by the viciousness of the apartheid system, Allan Boesak remains a prophet of reconciliation. He believes that it is incumbent upon Christians, both black and white, to keep uppermost in their minds the hope of living together in a new society based on justice and equality.

Allan Boesak was born in Somerset West, Cape Province, South Africa, in 1946. A product of the segregated school system and the constant oppression of blacks by whites, he grew up a victim of apartheid, yet one whose Christian upbringing instilled in him the strong conviction that a totally new social order could emerge, one based on the faith that "the gospel of Jesus Christ is the gospel of liberation" (*Farewell to Innocence*, p. 17). Allan's father, a primary school teacher, died when Allan was six years old. His mother worked as a seamstress to support the family. An experience important to his own sense of dignity was his discovery that the first Boesak, a member of the Khoikhoi tribe, had been a leader in a slave rebellion in South Africa. This disclosure helped him realize that his heritage was within a black family that took pride in its blackness.

Boesak attended the University of the Western Cape and the theological school at Belville. He later traveled to the United States where he studied at Union Theological Seminary in New York City and Colgate-Rochester Seminary. At Union Seminary, Boesak studied the writings of Martin Luther King, Jr., which further strengthened both his black pride and his advocacy of nonviolent resistance. In 1976 he received a doctorate in theology from the theological academy of Kampen in the Netherlands. While in Holland he wrote a series of essays comparing the ethical views of Martin Luther King, Jr., and Malcolm X. Since 1976 Boesak has been student chaplain at the University of the Western Cape, Peninsula Technical College, and at the Belville Training College for Teachers. He is a minister of the Dutch Reformed Mission church and in 1982 was elected president of the World Alliance of Reformed churches.

Boesak claims that a turning-point in his own life and in the lives of many black people of South Africa occurred in 1976, the year he took up his duties as college chaplain. On the 16th of June that year in Soweto, nearly 700 blacks were killed and hundreds more injured in rioting against the government, a revolt that soon spread to other parts of South Africa. This experience of violence and oppression was deepened in June 1980, when Boesak himself was present during the riots in Cape Town. He recalls: "For the first time in my life I was in the midst of violence. I saw young persons with nothing in their hands, marching in the streets to make clear to the government and the whites of South Africa: 'We do not want a heritage of hatred and racism and suspicion and mistrust in South Africa. We want to share with you our anguish for the future of this country we shall inherit, a country where we shall not be safe, where we shall not be able to live as human beings together. Let us change that.' And I saw these young persons teargassed; I saw them shot down with rifles'" (*Black and Reformed*, p. 44). Since 1980 Allan Boesak has come to increasing prominence as a major spokesperson for black theology and the rights of black people. His rhetoric has become more strident as he has denounced the white South African government for its continued support of the apartheid system, a government that believes that "God is white and he votes for the Nationalist Party" (*The Finger of God*, p. 92).

Boesak advocates a radical reconstruction of the South African government and social systems, and urges strong international economic sanctions against the government to force this radical reconstruction. He can be equally critical of the churches in South Africa for their failure to live up to the ideals of Jesus Christ. "How sick our country is! What we see on the outside—apartheid, humiliation, hatred, suspicion, the destruction of families, migrant labor—are merely the stinking boils on the surface, symptoms of all that is devouring us internally. Oppression, anxiety, suspicion, and mistrust all wreck our chances for authentic reconciliation. And in the meantime we remain mute before the misery and we argue in the press about whether women should wear hats in church!" (pp. 23-24).

Despite his increasingly strident attacks against the government and the white churches, Allan Boesak remains a prophet of reconciliation. But his notion of reconciliation is not the kind that only perpetuates inequality. Genuine reconciliation occurs, not between oppressor and oppressed, but between "persons who face each other in their authentic, vulnerable, and yet hopeful humanity"(p. 68), a union which involves total liberation and forgiveness. Boesak also seeks to build bridges between black theologians in South Africa who stress liberation from political, socioeconomic oppression and other African theologians who embrace cultural liberation. Boesak strongly believes it is important to include both emphases within the framework of a theology of liberation. In similar fashion he seeks for a rapproachement with Latin American liberation theologians as well as black theologians in North America. It is crucial that all of these groups work together in a common cause.

Boesak further insists that racism in South Africa is not the only issue. He declares: "While absolutely not minimizing racism as a demonic, pseudo-religious ideology (who, coming from South Africa, can?) we must nonetheless ask: Is racism the only *issue*? It seems to us that there is a far deeper malady in the American and South African societies that manifests itself in the form of racism" (*Farewell to Innocence*, p. 148). Boesak sees a direct link between racism and a capitalistic system which perpetuates deep social inequalities. But in attacking the social inequalities of capitalism Boesak by no means becomes a proponent of an unbridled socialism. Nor is he a disciple of Karl Marx. References in his writings to Marxism are scanty, to say the least. As noted earlier, what he does advocate is a totally new social order devoid of racial and social discrimination, one in which "one is only human because of others, with others, for others. This is black theology. It is authentic; it is worthwhile. It is, in the most profound sense of the word, gospel truth" (*Farewell to Innocence*, p. 152).

A distinctive feature of Allan Boesak's theology of liberation is his assertion that black theology is a reaffirmation of the Reformed tradition. He states: "It is my conviction that the reformed tradition has a future in this country only if black Reformed Christians are willing to take it up, make it truly their own, and let this tradition once again become what it once was: a champion of the cause of the poor and the oppressed, clinging to the confession of the lordship of Christ and to the supremacy of the word of God....I do not mean that we should accept everything in our tradition uncritically, for I indeed believe that black Christians should formulate a Reformed confession for our time and situation in our own words" (*Black and Reformed*, p. 95). Boesak believes that the Afrikaner version of the Reformed heritage is a distortion and backs up his argument with references to the teachings of John Calvin and to such church statements as the Heidelberg Catechism and Belgic Confession. He concludes: "The struggle in South Africa is not merely against an evil ideology; it is against a pseudo-religious ideology that was born in and continues to be justified out of the bosom of the Reformed churches" (p. 101). Here Boesak is making a major contribution as a Protestant theologian that parallels the thinking of many of his Roman Catholic colleagues, namely, that the theology of liberation is not a completely new phenomenon, but, rather, a reaffirmation of an important heritage in the Christian churches.

Allan Boesak is an apostle of hope in a sick society, one who can tell the proponents of apartheid to "go to hell" (*Black and Reformed*, p. 131), yet one whose faith in the gospel of Jesus Christ gives him cause for hope for eventual reconciliation between the races. His book *Walking on Thorns: The Call to Christian Obedience* is dedicated to young white friends in ND Sendingkerk who have joined the struggle for social justice. His book *Black and Reformed: Apartheid, Liberation and the Calvinist Tradition* is dedicated to another apostle of reconciliation: Desmond Tutu. In a sermon commemorating the Soweto riots, Allan Boesak used words reminiscent of another prophet of justice for blacks and whites, Martin Luther King, Jr.: "Let us believe that this land will one day be a land where we can live in peace with one another. Let us believe that this land will become a land where we will no longer be looked down upon because of the color of our skin" (*When Prayer Makes News*, p. 39).

BOOKS

Farewell to Innocence: A Socio-Ethical Study on Black Theology and Power. Maryknoll, N.Y.: Orbis Books, 1976.

The Finger of God: Sermons on Faith and Responsibility. Maryknoll, N.Y.: Orbis Books, 1982.

Walking on Thorns: The Call to Christian Obedience. Grand Rapids, Michigan: Eerdmans, 1984.

Black and Reformed: Apartheid, Liberation and the Calvinist Tradition. Maryknoll, N.Y.: Orbis Books, 1984.

When Prayer Makes News. Edited by Allan Boesak and Charles Villa-Vicencio. Philadelphia: The Westminster Press, 1986.

Comfort and Protest: Reflections on the Apocalypse of John of Patmos. Philadelphia: The Westminster Press, 1988.

MANAS BUTHELEZI

The point of departure for indigenous theology is not an eth-
nographically reconstructed worldview, but African people
themselves. When we speak of an "anthropological" ap-
proach we are thinking of the person, not as an object of
study—the theme of anthropology as a discipline—but as
God's creature who was entrusted with "dominion" over the
rest of creation. We are thinking, not of the 'colonial person'
who is the object of "dominion" by other people, a "black prob-
lem" to the white politicians, but a "post-colonial person"
who has been liberated by Christ from all that dehumanizes
(Toward Indigenous Theology in South Africa, p. 65).

In the continuing debate among African theologians over the issue of cultural liberation versus racial-economic liberation, Manas Buthelezi is a vigorous proponent of the latter. Blackness, not cultural setting, must be *the* basic criterion for African theology. Manas Buthelezi was born in South Africa in 1935. Educated at St. Francis College, he taught in a local high school for three years, during which time he received his undergraduate degree through a correspondence course from the University of South Africa in Pretoria. He studied at the Lutheran Seminary at Oscarsburg where he received his ministerial degree and was ordained a Lutheran pastor in 1961. Two years later, Buthelezi traveled to the United States where he earned a master's degree in theology at Yale Divinity School and, in 1968, his Ph.D. degree in theology from Drew University. It was during his years at Drew that Buthelezi first came in contact with the early stirrings of black theology in the United States, an exposure which would later become the basis for his own espousal of black theology in his native country.

Upon his return to South Africa, Buthelezi taught theology at the Lutheran Theological Seminary at Mapumolo and subsequently served as a Lutheran parish pastor in Sobantu, Pietermaritzburg. In 1972 he joined the staff of the Christian Institute as director of the Natal region. The Christian Institute had been established by Beyers Naudé in 1963 following the Sharpville massacre as a direct response to the evils of apartheid. During the 1970s both the Institute and Buthelezi himself became increasingly radicalized in their opposition to apartheid, and as a result encountered fierce opposition from the South African government. Buthelezi's publicly stated insistence that blacks had to take charge of their own destiny, even if this meant direct confrontation with the whites, led in 1973 to his being banned for five years under the Suppression of Communism Act. The ban was lifted after six months, however, because of Buthelezi's successful libel suit against the magazine *To The Point*, which had published an editorial accusing Buthelezi of threatening to assassinate South Africa's prime minister.

That same year Buthelezi, in a speech to the African Congress on Mission and Evangelism, declared that the Christian whites in South Africa had perverted the Christian gospel and that blacks must therefore take over leadership in evangelizing South Africa. After all, blacks were in the vast majority. After his brief stint with the Christian Institute, Buthelezi became Associate General

Secretary of the Federation of Evangelical Lutheran Churches in South Africa. In 1976 he further incurred the government's wrath when, following the Soweto riots, he became the leader of a group of blacks who set out to help the black victims cope with their suffering and and to publicize their plight. In 1977 Manas Buthelezi was consecrated Bishop of the Central Diocese of the Evangelical Church, a position he has held ever since. He has also served as President of the South African Council of Churches and has been a member both of the Commission on Studies of the Lutheran World Federation and the Commission on World Mission and Evangelism of the World Council of Churches.

Buthelezi distinguishes between two different approaches to African theology. The first, which he terms the *ethnographic*, takes as its point of departure the traditional African cultural worldview. Its goal is to translate the Christian faith into an African context, to retrieve Africa's past, to make Christianity indigenous. Buthelezi sees real dangers in this glorification of the past. He contends that it can be a romanticized way of ignoring the present-day ugly racial situation. It can become an opiate for the African people, lulling them into accepting their current oppressive state of life. In fact, Buthelezi goes so far as to suggest that it is the white missionaries who encourage this indigenous approach, which both placates the blacks and leads these white missionaries to think that they are in tune with modern times. Buthelezi writes: "There is a sense in which one can say that when the missionaries seem to be presumptuous in suggesting 'indigenous theology' to the African, they are strictly speaking looking for a solution to problems that stem from their own psychological 'hang-ups.' The suggestion here is that when the Africans seem to be encouraged to produce indigenous theology, they are just being used—as they have always been—to solve the psychological problems of the missionaries" (p. 63).

Buthelezi favors what he calls the *anthropological* approach by which he means that theology must emerge from today's existential situation. "Theology in Africa must reflect the throbbings of the life situation in which people find themselves" (p. 69). Buthelezi suggests what he calls a *theology of restlessness* which is not a flight back into the past, but a continual wrestling with the evils of today's social order. Theology must begin with today's problems, not yesterday's glories. Only this kind of theology will help blacks achieve their full liberation. "The black man must be enabled through the interpretation and application of the gospel to realize that blackness, like whiteness, is a good natural face cream from God and not some cosmological curse. Herein lies the contribution of Black Theology's methodological technique" ("An African Theology or a Black Theology?" p. 35).

In his vigorous advocacy of the anthropological approach, Buthelezi has come under attack, not only from Afrikaners and other proponents of apartheid, but also from those African theologians who believe that he denigrates the importance of cultural liberation. Kwesi Dickson, for example, faults Buthelezi for his negative attitude toward cultural indigenization. Dickson argues: "Surely the traditional religio-cultural ideas and values have a part to play in establishing the humanity of the African population in South Africa; they could provide a booster to the determination of the African population to seek an end to the iniquitous system under which they live" (*Theology in Africa*, p. 138).

Buthelezi remains adamant that racism and its ugly manifestation in apartheid must be the central issue for African theology. Even the churches are so infected with the idol of racism that God may have to "use forces outside the church in order to liberate the church....The church will be the last bastion of racism in a liberated South Africa. Those who can no longer practice racism in politics, economy and in social life will flee to the church and practice it under the guise of freedom of religion" ("Church Unity and Human Divisions of Racism," pp. 425-426).

If Manas Buthelezi is correct in his assessment, it is little wonder that he is suspicious of any theological approach that might lessen the urgency of confronting the issue of racism. "At this moment in South African history the suffering of the black people is becoming redemptive. The black people are now regarding their suffering as a step towards liberation instead of a pool of fate and self-pity. Right in the midst of the experience of suffering, the black people have made themselves believe that they can do something about their own liberation" ("Daring to Live for Christ," p. 180).

By no means a supporter of the South African government, Buthelezi has not in recent years been nearly as vocal in his opposition as Desmond Tutu and Allan Boesak. His reluctance to become actively involved in social protest has caused considerable friction in his own religious community, particularly among younger Lutheran pastors. One reason for his moderate approach may be an accommodation he has reached with his conservative first cousin, Zulu Chief Gatsha Buthelezi. Whatever the reason, Manas Buthelezi is no longer the militant leader that he was.

ARTICLES

"Change in the Church," *South African Outlook*, August 1973.

"Christianity in South Africa," *CI News*, June 1973.

"Black Theology in Bangkok: Relevance for South Africa," *South African Outlook*, October 1974.

"An African Theology or a Black Theology?," *Black Theology: The South African Voice*. Edited by Basil Moore. London: C. Hurst and Co., 1973, pp. 29-36.

"The Christian Institute and Black South Africa," *South African Outlook*, October 1974.

"Daring to Live for Christ," *Mission Trends No. 3: Third World Theologies*. Edited by Gerald H. Anderson and Thomas F. Stransky. Grand Rapids, Michigan: Eerdmans, 1976, pp. 176-180.

"Towards Indigenous Theology in South Africa," *The Emergent Gospel: Theology from the Underside of History*. Edited by Sergio Torres and Virginia Fabella. Maryknoll, N.Y.: Orbis Books, 1978, pp. 56-76.

"Church Unity and Human Divisions of Racism," *International Review of Mission*, Vol. 73, No. 292, October 1984, pp. 419-426.

KWESI A. DICKSON

It is essential that African Christians should be in a position to express in a vital way what Christ means to them and to do so in and through a cultural medium that makes original thinking possible. Let Christ call them, rebuke them, accept them in his embrace; let him chasten them and carry them in his arms—but let all this be done in a medium that will give Christ's approach an eternal impact. The faith can be meaningful only when Christ is encountered as speaking and acting authentically, when he is heard in the African language, when culture shapes the human voice that answers the voice of Christ. To put this in another way, Christ must be heard to speak to African Christians direct (Theology in Africa, pp. 4-5).

24

Kwesi Dickson believes that the Christian faith can no longer be a Western import into Africa. African theology must do justice to the life-circumstances of the Africans. Dickson's chief concern, then, is to place Christianity into an authentically African cultural context.

Dickson was born in Saltpond, Ghana, in 1929, the son of a Methodist minister. At that time the Methodist Church and the educational system in Ghana reflected the British model. Yet Dickson's father believed it important that his children should maintain their African roots. So, for example, the father did not give his son an English first name, an unusual gesture in view of the common practice that at a child's baptism one would normally be given a "Christian," i.e., Western name. Dickson's father also composed many hymns in his native African language.

Dickson received his undergraduate degree at the University College of the Gold Coast in 1956, his bachelor of divinity degree in London and a bachelor of letters from Oxford University in 1959, specializing in the Old Testament. During his undergraduate and graduate years he became more and more aware of how "foreign" the educational system was in terms of course content. As a result Dickson found himself increasingly drawn to the conviction that African theology must forego its Western bias and become more closely tied in with the African religious-cultural traditions. To be sure, there had been talk previously of the need for indigeniza-tion. But the tendency in these earlier days was simply to put "an African cultural sheen on European theology."

Between 1960 and 1980 Dickson served as Lecturer, then Professor and finally Head of the Department for the Study of Religions at the University of Ghana. During the academic year 1978-79, he was the Henry Luce Visiting Professor of World Christianity at Union Theological Seminary in New York City. Since 1980 he has been Director of the Institute of African Studies at the University of Ghana. Dickson's lifelong interest has been to underscore the im-perative need for an African cultural theology, a theology that ad-dresses African concerns in a way that Africans can readily under-stand. In some circles African theology is understood simply as a matter of replacing Western cultural incidentals with African or-naments. But Dickson sees the problem as a far deeper one. He ad-vocates the total rethinking of the Christian faith which will end up as a full-fledged propositional articulation of African theology.

Dickson's major book is *Theology in Africa*, the most sustained exposition of theology in a thoroughly African setting. As he himself suggests: "The writing of this book was prompted in part by the conviction that there is a need to create more discussion and thereby, hopefully, to embroil the Church in Africa, particularly the historic churches, in the task of re-examining the inherited expressions of faith in Christ" (p. 8). Dickson takes pains to make a careful distinction between liberation theology and African theology. For him liberation theology in Africa is primarily a South African phenomenon, closely identified with Latin American liberation theology and American black theology. He criticizes its excesses, faulting it for its seemingly exclusive focus upon practical action derived from its preoccupation with political, economic, and social issues at the expense of the cultural dimension. African theology, on the other hand, insists that the role of African culture is absolutely indispensable in forging an authentic theology for that continent.

To be sure, Dickson is well aware of the ambiguity of the term "African theology" and the danger of so over-emphasizing the cultural setting that social issues are neglected. But he unabashedly admits that his primary interests lie in the cultural phenomena and he pleads for a multi-pronged approach which recognizes the rich diversity of the African continent. He writes: "Africa is a continent which presents a varied religious, social, economic, political, racial and cultural picture, and it should not be surprising that different theological emphases should exist. Thus it is true that, by and large, African theologians outside South Africa have tended to keep socio-economic and political matters out of all discussion of theology" (*Theology in Africa*, pp. 131-132).

In arguing for the importance of the cultural dimension, Dickson points out that outside South Africa most of black Africa is ruled by black Africans. He notes that these countries have achieved their independence from white colonial domination. Whites simply are not able to oppress blacks as they do in South Africa. Dickson also insists that the recovery of Africa's cultural past will reveal many parallels with the aspirations of South African black theology. He notes, for example, that in traditional African societies there has been a deep concern for building a just social order. Oppression of any segment of society has been frowned upon. So Dickson believes that the retrieval of African culture will provide important ammunition for South African black theologians in their battle against white racism and oppression. In short, Dickson stresses that his cultural approach embraces a far wider view of Africa than does African black theology.

Dickson also makes the point that a strong emphasis on the cultural factors that shape African life will lead to a drastic reshaping of African theological education. If African theology is to be done in specifically African contexts, then education must reflect these contexts in its language, symbols, and even beliefs. Theological education will, of necessity, have to include a study of African history, sociology, political science, native religion and all those other areas that have a direct bearing on African life. He warns against slurring over these broader areas of African life, lest one be guilty of "oversimplifying the issue of the poor, to the extent of making its concern faddish" (*Theology in Africa*, p. 225). He further suggests that the poor have a major responsibility in retrieving their own heritage. Failing to do this will only contribute to their own impoverishment.

Marxism plays no role whatsoever in Dickson's thinking. He says that he is "allergic" to ideologies that have been developed in cultural contexts outside Africa and then imported for African consumption. For the same reason he says that Latin American liberation theology cannot be the model for African theology. Africans must forge their own distinctive convictions. Kwesi Dickson believes that his distinctive mission is to retrieve the African heritage, to save African theology from foreigners. If this can be accomplished, he predicts that the end result will be tantamount to an explosion in reshaping the content and form of the Christian faith.

BOOKS

Akan Religion and the Christian Faith. Edited by Kwesi Dickson. Ghana University Press, 1965.

Biblical Revelation and African Beliefs. Co-edited with Paul Ellingworth. London: Lutterworth Press, 1969.

Aspects of Religion and Life in Africa, The J. B. Danquah Memorial Lectures, 10th Series, Ghana Academy of Arts and Sciences, 1977.

Theology in Africa. Maryknoll, N.Y.: Orbis Books, 1984.

ARTICLES

"Christian and African Traditional Ceremonies," *Practical Anthropology,* Vol. 18, No. 2, March-April 1971, pp. 64-71.

"Hebrewisms of West Africa: The Old Testament and African Life and Thought," *Legon Journal of Humanities,* Vol. 1, 1974, pp. 23-33.

"African Theology—Whence Methodology and Content," *Howard Journal of Religious Thought,* Vol. 33, Fall-Winter, 1975.

"Continuity and Discontinuity between The Old Testament and African Life and Thought," *African Theology En Route.* Edited by Kofi Appiah-Kubi and Sergio Torres. Maryknoll, N.Y.: Orbis Books, 1979, pp. 95-108.

EDWARD W. FASHOLE-LUKE

The quest for African Christian theologies...amounts to attempting to make clear the fact that conversion to Christianity must be coupled with cultural continuity. Furthermore, if Christianity is to change its status from that of resident alien to that of citizen, then it must become incarnate in the life and thought of Africa, and its theologies must bear the distinctive stamp of mature African thinking and reflection. What African theologians have been endeavoring to do is to draw together the various and disparate sources which make up the total religious experience of Christians in Africa into a coherent and meaningful pattern (The Quest for African Christian Theologies, *p. 146).*

Edward Fashole-Luke believes it important not only that African Christian theology should come to positive terms with the African cultural setting, but also should seek reconciliation between blacks and whites, between the oppressed and the oppressor.

Fashole-Luke was born in Freetown, Sierra Leone, in 1934. He attended Fourah Bay College, receiving his B.A. in general studies in 1959. Upon graduation, he traveled to England where he earned his B.A. degree in theology from St. John's College in Durham, in 1963. During his years in Durham he was ordained an Anglican priest in the Durham Cathedral and served in the parish of St. Cuthbert and St. Aldah. He received his Ph.D. in theology from King's College, Aberdeen, Scotland, in 1969. He then returned to his native country, and since 1969 he has taught theology at Fourah Bay College. In 1985 he was appointed senior chaplain there. For the past two decades he has been continually involved in ecumenical conferences related to theological issues, planned parenthood, and women's ordination.

Fashole-Luke's major interests have been in African traditional religion and the impact that Christianity and Islam have had on native African beliefs and practices, especially among the Creoles of Sierra Leone. His continuing interest in biblical and patristic studies—his doctoral dissertation was on "The Doctrine of the Church in the Writings of St. Cyprian of Carthage"—has also deepened his appreciation for the heritage of African Christianity. He has made an extensive study of the writings of St. Augustine and the North African churches of the early Christian era, and how these churches adapted to their cultural context. He is interested in discovering resources and models that may be helpful for today's African churches. Two of his published articles reflect this interest: "St. Augustine and the North African Church: A Typology for the Modern African Church," and "The Relevance of Early Church History for Training for the Ministry in West Africa."

In his concern to relate the Christian gospel to the social and political setting in West Africa, Fashole-Luke has not hesitated to criticize Western missionaries whose provincial theological training has led them to divorce Christianity from the African heritage, thereby forcing converts to make a sharp break with their past. It is primarily for this reason, he points out, that the African independent churches have flourished as an important way of preserving the African's identity. To be sure, Fashole-Luke recognizes the problem of regarding the Bible as the prime authority and Jesus as unique, while at the same time defending the intrinsic value of native religion. The point is that Christianity can only make sense in terms the native people can understand and assimilate. "We must therefore theologize primarily for our own local communities" ("The Quest for African Christian Theologies," p. 145). Fashole-Luke notes with approval how in the past decade research into native African religions has moved from generalized continent-wide studies to a more concentrated attention on local communities. Cultural continuity between Christianity and each tribe and village is, for him, the key issue.

But if Fashole-Luke can be critical of white missionaries for espousing cultural discontinuity, he can be equally critical of some South African black theologians for too much emphasis on racial and political issues to the exclusion of cultural liberation. He writes: "In the Republic of South Africa, African theology is equated with black theology and the emphasis on blackness indicates the ethnic implications of the task; considerable attention is given there to the exposition of the gospel in terms of liberation from political, social and economic issues....It is surely at this critical point that African theologians are challenged by the gospel to raise African Christian theologies above the level of ethnic or racial categories" (p. 147). Harmonious living between blacks and whites in a just society is an important goal for Fashole-Luke, a goal which will never be achieved if blackness is the ultimate criterion. When asked why through the years he has held on to reconciliation rather than blackness as the cornerstone of his theology, he replied: "My ideas and thoughts have been shaped by Harry Sawyerr, my former teacher at Fourah Bay College and Charles Cranfield, my former tutor at the University of Durham, England. It is perhaps this combination of the white and black keys of the piano to produce harmony that has led to my suspicion about the creation of black theologies or any ethnic theologies."

It should be pointed out that this concentration on the theme of reconciliation does not mean that for Fashole-Luke social and political problems are unimportant. Quite the contrary. He warns Christians in the independent states of Africa that they must never neglect these issues. Unfortunately, many Africans outside of South Africa "fail to see the oppression of blacks by blacks in their own countries. In many independent states, military regimes rule and are kept in power by sheer brute force" (*Christianity in Independent Africa*, p. 359). Fashole-Luke envisions an all-embracing theology of liberation that is larger than any one issue or set of issues. For this reason he can assert that "African independent states need theologies of liberation as much as, if not more than, the blacks in the occupied territories of southern Africa" (p. 359). Marxism plays no role in Fashole-Luke's theological thinking. Indeed Fashole-Luke believes that Marxism, wherever it has become dominant in a society, has turned out to be a negative force. "Social analysis may be a necessary prerequisite for theologizing, but it must not be tied to the apron strings of an economic analysis of society which has everywhere proved to be subversive of personal liberty and the impoverishment of the citizens of the so-called socialist countries."

In short, Fashole-Luke is a proponent of the dominant theme of reconciliation. He opposes the "abrasiveness" of South African black theology and the imperialistic attitudes of many western missionaries. He wants to help shape an African theology for the African people themselves without losing appreciation for western theological contributions. Cultural continuity is his norm, but it is not to be espoused at the expense of political and social concerns. In Fashole-Luke's words, this search for authentic African Christian theologies "should be looked upon as a medium by which Africans and non-Africans can think together about the fundamental articles of the Christian faith in Africa. The quest must therefore be ecumenical and all inclusive" ("The Quest for African Christian Theologies," p. 148).

BOOKS

New Testament Christianity for Africa and the World. Edited by M.E. Glasswell and E. W. Fashole-Luke. London: S.P.C.K., 1974.

Christianity in Independent Africa. Edited by E. W. Fashole-Luke, R. Gray, A. Hastings and G. Tasie. Bloomington, Indiana: Indiana University Press, 1978.

ARTICLES

"St. Augustine and the North African Church: A Typology for the Modern African Church?" *African Historical Studies,* Vol. 3, No. 2, 1970, pp. 443-448.

"An African Indigenous Theology: Fact or Fiction?" *Sierre Leone Bulletin of Religion,* Vol. 11, 1971, pp. 1-15.

"What Is African Christian Theology?" *African Ecclesiastical Review,* 1974, pp. 383-388.

"The Quest for African Christian Theologies," *Mission Trends No. 3: Third World Theologies.* Edited by Gerald H. Anderson and Thomas F. Stransky. Grand Rapids, Michigan: Wm. B. Eerdmans, 1976, pp. 135-151.

"The Relevance of Early Church History for Training for the Ministry in West Africa," Freetown, 1977, pp. 72-79.

"Footpaths and Signposts to African Christian Theologies," *Scottish Journal of Theology,* Vol. 46, No. 4, October 1981, pp. 54-78.

JOHN S. MBITI

The God described in the Bible is none other than the God who is already known in the framework of our traditional African religiosity. The missionaries who introduced the gospel to Africa in the past 200 years did not bring God to our continent. Instead, God brought them. They proclaimed the name of Jesus Christ. But they used the names of the God who was and is already known by African peoples—such as Mungu, Mulungu, Katonda, Ngai—and thousands more. These were not empty names. They were names of one and the same God, the creator of the world, the father of our Lord Jesus Christ (The Encounter of Christian Faith and African Religion, *p. 55*).

John S. Mbiti has richly enhanced African theology in challenging the traditional Western distinction between general and special revelations with his insistence that God can be found in African religious traditions as much as God is revealed in the Judeo-Christian tradition.

John Mbiti was born in Kitui, Kenya, in 1931. He remembers vividly from his boyhood in Kenya how he was imbued with the widely held conviction that the Christian faith as imported from the West had an exclusive claim to truth and that, in comparison, native African religions were all false and heathen. He attended Makerere University in Uganda and later Barrington College in Rhode Island where he received A.B. and Th.B. degrees. He completed his Ph.D. degree at Cambridge in 1963, specializing in biblical studies. His undergraduate and graduate studies only served to reinforce the traditional Western Christian bias against African native religions.

After serving in a parish in England, Mbiti returned to Makerere University to teach both New Testament and African religions and remained there from 1964 to 1974. From 1974 to 1980, he served as Director and Professor at the Ecumenical Institute in Bossey, Switzerland, and for six years was Director of the Ecumenical Institute of the World Council of Churches in Geneva. He has held visiting professorships at Union Theological Seminary and Harvard University; at Lausanne, Fribourg, Geneva and Zurich Universities in Switzerland; and at Bayreuth in West Germany. He is a parish minister at Burgdorf, Switzerland, and teaches Missiology and Extra-European Theology at the University of Bern.

During his early years of teaching both the Bible and African religions at the University of Makerere, Mbiti did extensive research on African religion, with special emphasis on tribal conceptions of God. He soon came to the conclusion that Africans had been and still were "notoriously religious." He also learned that most African Christians still identified with their native religious beliefs and customs, which had come down to them through oral tradition. He began to challenge the long-held prejudice that these native beliefs and customs were inherently worthless. His books *African Religion and Philosophy* (1969) and *Concepts of God in Africa* (1970) were pioneering efforts, pointing out the tremendous diversity of religious beliefs and practices among the more than a thousand African tribes. Yet Mbiti also noted a certain commonality within this rich diversity, and, most important, challenged the long held Western insistence that God had been revealed in a saving way only through the Western Judeo-Christian tradition. He argued for the authenticity and truth-value of African religion.

During the past two decades, Mbiti has been a prolific writer on African religion. His book *The Prayers of African Religion* (1975) is a compendium of over three hundred prayers, prayers that he discovered were usually directed both to the supreme God and to the innumerable spirits "thronging together like swarming mosquitoes in the evening," spirits that continue to play a large role in African religion. His book *Bible and Theology in African Christianity* (1986) reiterates his basic conviction that the Christian faith today must be expressed in African terms. In this work he echoes Kwesi A. Dickson's contention that God is God of all peoples; that God was revealed in African religion long before Western Christian missionaries brought their faith to the African shores. The fact that Mbiti has taught and carried on research both in the Bible and in African religions has helped him to see the many similarities between the two areas. This is why he argues forcefully for a continuing creative interchange between the two disciplines. Yet he insists that the African religious traditions can never become a substitute for the Bible. He believes that the Bible remains a distinctive, even primary, but not exclusive, authority for the Christian faith.

It should be pointed out that John Mbiti does not consider himself to be a liberation theologian. He is adamant on this point. His reasons for this assertion are twofold. First, he faults liberation theologians—and here he identifies liberation theology primarily with South African and North American black theologies—for their lack of a strong biblical tradition. He says that liberation theologians have such an excessive preoccupation with liberation that they seem to use the Bible only when it confirms their liberation theme. There is much more to the Bible than those passages which support liberation theology! If liberation theologians refuse to admit this simple fact, they will only lose their credibility.

Second, he criticizes black theologians in South Africa and North America for making an ideology out of blackness. These theologians are only cutting themselves off from equally important themes when they idolatrize blackness. Mbiti writes: "African theology has no interest in coloring God or Christ black, no interest in reading liberation into every text, no interest in telling people to think or act 'black' " ("An African Views American Black Theology," p. 479).

Here we note Mbiti's affinity with other African theologians outside of South Africa who show a greater interest in the African cultural context than the issue of race. Yet surely Mbiti and these other African theologians meet the *spirit* of liberation theology in their intense concern for the indigenization of Christianity, their insistence that the Christian faith must be radically reinterpreted in terms of its various African cultural settings. In an important article, "Christianity Tilts to the South: A New Challenge for Christian Ministry and Theological Education," Mbiti points out how a statistical balance of Christians between the northern and southern hemispheres was reached in the 1980s and that the scales continue to tilt more and more to the south. As a result the time has come to "do theology in the hundreds of southern languages." Mbiti argues: "The challenge is whether we Christians of the south can evolve a kind of ecumenical sharing of suffering and hope....How can we communicate what it means to study theology with an empty stomach, while our counterparts in the north study it with stomachs bulging from big meals or layers of fatness?" (p. 8). Mbiti may not wish to count himself among the liberation theologians, but both his concerns and his rhetoric often dovetail with theirs. Moreover, he has attended meetings of the Ecumenical Association of Third World Theologians, comprised mainly of liberation theologians, and has addressed these gatherings.

Marxism plays no part in Mbiti's theology. This perhaps reflects his apparent lack of interest in developing a sustained critique of the social-economic-political issues. John Mbiti's major contribution to theology and to biblical studies has been his pioneering and continuing concern for the importance of native African religions and for his insistence that the biblical faith in Africa be experienced and expressed in the African context.

BOOKS

African Religions and Philosophy. New York: Praeger, 1969.

Concepts of God in Africa. New York: Praeger, 1970.

New Testament Eschatology in an African Background. New York: Oxford University Press, 1971.

The Prayers of African Religion. Maryknoll, N.Y.: Orbis Books, 1976.

Bible and Theology in African Christianity. New York: Oxford University Press, 1986.

ARTICLES

"Christianity and Traditional Religions in Africa," *International Review of Mission*, Vol. 59, No. 236, Oct. 1970, World Council of Churches, Geneva, pp. 430-440.

"African Theology," *Worldview*, Vol. 16, No. 8, August 1973, pp. 33-39

"An African Views American Black Theology," *Black Theology: A Documentary History*, 1966-1979. Edited by Gayraud Wilmore and James Cone. Maryknoll, N.Y.: Orbis Books, 1979, pp. 477-482.

"Some Current Concerns of African Theology," *The Expository Times*, Vol. 87, No. 6, March 1976, pp. 164-168.

"The Biblical Basis in Present Trends of African Theology,", *African Theology En Route*. Edited by Kofi Appiah-Kubi and Sergio Torres. Maryknoll, N.Y.: Orbis Books, 1979, pp. 83-95.

"The Future of Christianity in Africa," *Cross Currents*, Vol. 28, No. 4, Winter 1978-79, pp. 387-394.

"The Encounter of Christian Faith and African Religion," *Theologians in Transition*. Edited by James Wall. New York: Crossroad, 1981, pp. 53-59.

"Christianity Tilts to the South: A New Challenge for Christian Ministry and Theological Education," *The Indian Journal of Theology*, Vol. 33, Nos. 1, 2 & 3, January - September, 1984.

EMMANUEL MILINGO

*What is special at a healing session, and what has at-
tracted many people, is the presence of God. It is special
because here the sick experience Him through their physical as well as their spiritual being....There is a loving
closeness between each and every one of us. Here then is
proved the fact that God is love, God is unity, God is Father to all of us* (The World in Between, p. 27).

Emmanuel Milingo's unique offering to Third World theology has been his advocacy of the healing powers of God as a means of liberating human beings from selfishness and from evil powers. He finds this emphasis on faith healing to be strongly imbedded in African spirituality and believes it essential for the Christian faith to incorporate this important African heritage.

Milingo was born in 1930 in Mukwa in the eastern part of Zambia. He is a descendent of the Zambian Nguni, an offshoot of the Zulus. His early years were spent helping his father herd the family cattle. At the tender age of twelve he enrolled in a private mission school, The Society of Our Lady of Africa, which was founded by French Catholic missionaries. The story is told that his name was originally Lotte, but that he was so put off by the biblical story of Lot that he changed his name to Emmanuel. Milingo was strongly attached to his mother; and when she died at an early age, he transferred his attention to the Virgin Mary; and from that point he gradually developed his later deeply-held conviction that God must be considered Mother as well as Father. Milingo continued his schooling under church auspices and eventually decided to become a priest. He was ordained in 1958.

After serving in a parish in Zambia for two years, Milingo studied for a year at the Institute of Pastoral Sociology in Rome and then continued his studies at University College in Dublin, Ireland, where he received a graduate degree in education. He served for a year as a parish priest in the diocese of Chipata in his native country; and in 1966 settled in Lusaka as Secretary for Communications of the Zambia Episcopal Conference. To improve his communication skills, Milingo took a course in radio preaching at Nairobi and soon thereafter began a career as a "radio priest." As a result of his radio ministry he gained a large following throughout Zambia.

During this period of his life, Milingo began to develop an intense interest in native African religions, especially as they reflected African spirituality. He also turned his attention to the poor people of Lusaka. In that capacity he soon saw the need for a theology of liberation that emerged from the poor and served the needs of the poor. Then in 1969, at the age of thirty-nine, Emmanuel Milingo was consecrated Archbishop of Lusaka by Pope Paul VI.

The major turning point in Milingo's life occurred in 1973 when, quite by accident, he discovered that God had given him the gift of healing. On this particular occasion a woman came to him, complaining that for the past several years she was hearing voices and, as a result, was so afraid she could not eat. In ministering to her Milingo received a vision that ordered him to tell her to go to sleep so he could speak directly with her soul. This he did, and her recovery was instantaneous. As Milingo relates it: "I can remember a great deal that happened in the month of May 1973. I know that the Lord was leading me to the healing of the disease of which many of my fellow Zambians are victims—mashawe" (*The World in Between*, p. 15). In July of that year he reported this healing incident to a Catholic Action group at the cathedral. He also told them that he believed that the Catholic church could heal the mashawe disease by means of the power of healing; and he encouraged his listeners to bring victims who were suffering from this disease to him to be healed. That is how Milingo began the practice of public faith healing, a practice to which he gave increasing attention.

To be sure, belief in spirit-possession and the practice of being exorcised from the clutches of the devil is by no means unique to Africa. Yet it is a practice that is deeply imbedded in African native religions. Milingo considers it to be a ministry of deliverance whereby suffering souls are quite literally delivered from the control of evil spirits. It is a conviction closely related to the African belief in ancestor worship whereby many Africans devoutly believe that they can communicate directly with their deceased ancestors who will then help them. This closely resembles belief in guardian angels, a concept which is so much a part of Catholic tradition. Milingo writes: "The fact is that there is never a time when I am alone, even as I am speaking now. I am in the company of many guardians whose ranks I don't know. I am grateful to them all, for they have protected me on several occasions from the evil spirits and the spirits of revenge. They have been at my side as I traveled to distant places and lands. They are immediately at my side when I call upon them" (p. 120).

Milingo believes it very important for the Catholic church to incorporate the deep insights of African spirituality, especially insofar as they pertain to the gift of healing. For Milingo, God is both Mother and Father, the One who gives birth to all of creation. Jesus is the great Ancestor in the hierarchy of the spirit world, the chief intercessor between God and humanity. It is important, Milingo says, that we "marry Jesus with our ancestors," experiencing his living presence in the same way that our ancestors continue to live and exert their influence over human beings. The sacrament of baptism becomes a means of deliverance from the evil spirits; and the sacrament of penance becomes a confession of the rejection of the power of Satan and the acceptance of the forgiving, healing powers of the Ancestor Jesus. In short, Milingo is a strong proponent of the importance of making Christianity indigenous to the African belief-structure, that "taking the Africans with their beliefs into Christianity is a necessary step on the way to their full conversion" (*The World in Between*, p. 85).

Since he discovered that he had the gift of healing in 1973, Emmanuel Milingo has expanded his healing ministry into a worldwide mission through speaking and writing. As a result he has come into increasing conflict with church authorities. In years past and present, these authorities have dismissed so much of native African religion as animistic and not authentically Christian (which usually means Western). In his own diocese of Lusaka, many of his fellow priests, most of them educated in the West, began to criticize him for exploiting the practice of exorcism to rid the sick of evil spirits. In 1982, Milingo was ordered to report to the Vatican. There he met with the Congregation for the Propagation of the Faith. He was told not to appear in public or attend any healing services. Not only was he closely examined for possible heretical views, but he was subjected to psychiatric tests to insure his mental fitness. He was also charged with the misuse of diocesan funds, a charge that he was never allowed to rebut. For a period of a year and a half he was forced to remain in Rome and was under constant pressure to resign as Archbishop of Lusaka on the grounds that he could not be both an archbishop and a faith healer. He consistently replied that he would not even consider resigning until he had the opportunity to discuss his situation with Pope John Paul II. A papal audience was finally granted and Milingo resigned his archbishopric in order to avoid further dissension in his diocese. In return, Pope John Paul II permitted him to resume his healing ministry and no longer confined him to Rome. The Pope also appointed him special delegate to the Pontifical Commission for Migration and Tourism. Milingo today continues his healing mission on a worldwide basis.

Emmanuel Milingo adds a special twist to the theology of liberation of the Third World. His healing ministry provides a unique appeal to the poor and oppressed who suffer from diseases, both physical and mental. They find liberation by means of the power of healing which Milingo believes is a direct gift to him from God. "The aim of Christianity," Milingo testifies, "is to open wide our eyes to the generosity of God to us, and to give us strength to combat the evils and adversities which make it hard for us to pursue the good shown us by God" (p. 94).

BOOKS AND PAMPHLETS

Healing. Lusaka, 1976.

Black Civilization and the Catholic Church. Abidjan, Ivory Coast, 1977.

The Church of the Spirits. Lusaka, 1978.

Precautions in the Ministry of Healing. Moshi, Tanzania, 1978.

Father, Son and Holy Spirit. Lusaka, 1981.

My Prayers Are Not Heard. Rome, 1982.

The World in Between: Christian Healing and the Struggle for Spiritual Survival. Maryknoll, N. Y.: Orbis Books, 1984.

ENGELBERT MVENG

Strange, is it not, that in the immense literature that we have on the poor today, Africa is always looked upon and derided? There is a type of poverty that I call 'anthropological poverty.' It consists in despoiling human beings not only of what they have, but of everything that constitutes their being and essence—their identity, history, ethnic roots, language, culture, faith, creativity, dignity, pride, ambitions, right to speak...we could go on indefinitely (Third World Theology—What Theology? What Third World? *p. 220).*

Engelbert Mveng's principal bestowal on Third World liberation theology has been his introduction of the concept of "anthropological impoverishment," the idea that the First World has literally stripped Africans of their personhood, negating everything that is distinctively African in their personal lives. The first thing that Africans must do, Mveng contends, is to regain their pride and dignity by affirming everything that constitutes their "being and essence."

Mveng was born in Enam-Ngal, commune of Ngulmakong, Cameroon, in 1930. A product of the local school system where he experienced racial discrimination firsthand, in the early fifties he spent a period of three years in the novitiate of Djuna in the Belgian Congo. After studying at the Minor Seminary of Akono in the Diocese of Yaounde, Cameroon, and the Major Seminary in Otele, Mveng traveled to Europe for extensive graduate training. He studied at Faculté de Philosophie et Lettres de Namur in Belgium and earned licentiates at the Universities of Louvain and Lyon. He was ordained a Jesuit priest at Lyon in 1963. For the next decade he traveled back and forth between Africa and Europe. For two years he taught Greek at the College Libermann in Doulay, Cameroon, and in 1969 he earned certificates in Latin and Greek at the University of Dakar. The following year he completed his doctoral work at the Sorbonne where his dissertation topic was "The Greek Sources of Black African History from Homer to Strabo."

Mveng's professional career has been as rich and varied as his academic training. Since 1965 he has intermittently been professor of history at the University of Yaounde, becoming Chair of the Department in 1984. However, for a period of three years (1974 to 1977), he lived in Nigeria, supervising the preparations for the Second World Festival of Black African Arts. He has also held several other important positions, including Head of the Department of Cultural Affairs in the Ministry of Education and Culture in Yaounde, Secretary General of the Panafrican Movement of Christian Intellectuals, Secretary General of the Ecumenical Association of African Theologians, President of the Cameroon National Committee for Church History, and founder and director of the Black Art Workshop in Yaounde.

Mveng's eclectic academic and professional interests have served to give him an expansive view of liberation. He has long been associated with a group which he helped to establish in Yaounde, the Community of the Beatitudes, set up to train priests, nuns, and lay brothers for service in the Third World. Its primary goal is to "share the life of the 'people of the beatitudes,' and to proclaim the gospel of liberation to the people of our time. We receive members from Africa, from the Third World, and also from the First World" ("An African Experience," p. 397).

With respect to the First World, Mveng believes that the time has come for the Third World to liberate the First World from the imprisonment of exploitation, money, and arrogance. He exclaims: "Please accept the gospel of Jesus Christ from the poor, the powerless and the oppressed of the world" (p. 397). The converse side of this process is that Africans must liberate themselves from their "anthropological impoverishment," a total liberation which for Mveng includes art and history as well as theology and spirituality. Here Mveng's experience as a black Christian artist plays a large role. He himself has produced many pieces of African Christian art, for example, in the Cathedral of Yaounde and in the Basilica of Nazareth in Israel. Mveng believes that art establishes an important link between human life and the cosmos. Art is in its own way religious language with its own rich signs and symbols. These convey the essential themes of human existence: life, suffering, joy and death, as a celebration of the mysteries and wonders of God's creation. Mveng is unusual in that his research and personal interests have included history, art, anthropology, theology, spirituality, and the Bible, all of which must be seen as essential to the liberation of Africans from their anthropological impoverishment.

In his expansive view of liberation for Africa, Mveng has not only expressed impatience with First World theologians for their cultural imperialism. He has also been critical of Third World theologians from Latin America for their imperialism. He claims that the Ecumenical Association of Third World Liberation Theologians (EATWOT) was originally an African inspiration "born in Louvain, of confrontation and dialogue among young African theologians (its inspirers) in company with their Belgian, Latin American, and Asian colleagues" ("Third World Theology—What Theology? What Third World?" p. 217). Yet, despite its African origin, the Latin American members of EATWOT have often shunned their African colleagues. Mvent insists that "Africa is not taken seriously. Even in the Third World itself, in an association of theologians, Africa remains the everlastingly marginalized—not to say forgotten!—continent." (p. 218). Mveng points out that in most cases Latin American theologians do not even represent the minority groups of their own continent: the blacks, the native peoples, and so on. "How shall we fashion a theology of the Third World without them? What kind of 'Third World theology' would we have if it were a theology they would not recognize?" (p. 218). Mveng concludes that for Africa liberation theology cannot be imported from other parts of the Third World any more than it can from Europe and North America. "We Africans are existentially and tragically alone. No one can do our encounter with Christ for us. Nor can anyone else take responsibility for what we do, because we believe we must" (p. 219).

Mveng believes that since Marxism is in origin a western phenomenon, it has little value in the African setting. Marxism may be useful in a capitalist context, for example, in Latin America. But "Marxism has no answer to the apartheid system of South Africa, not even to the anthropological impoverishment of Black Africa. The problem of Racism and Imperialism has no adequate solution within the Marxist system." Mveng can not understand why many critics of Third World liberation theology seem to suggest a necessary link between Marxism and liberation theology. They are as wrong on this score as they are in lumping together Latin American, Asian, and African theologies of liberation.

Virtually all of Engelbert Mveng's books have been published in French and to date only one has been translated into English. This means that he has not received the attention he deserves in the United States and other English-speaking nations. His concept of theological impoverishment is crucial, not only in establishing an important link between the proponents of racial-social-economic liberation and those who stress cultural liberation, but also in providing such a rich view of the latter. His experience as an artist provides an added ingredient for African liberation theology, thereby helping to transcend "the universal derision that has always accompanied the 'civilized' world's discourse upon and encounter with Africa—and still accompanies it today" ("Third World Liberation Theology—What Theology? What Third World?" p. 220).

BOOKS

Take Up Your Cross: Meditations on the Way of the Cross. London: Geoffrey Chapman, 1963.

L'Afrique dans l'Eglise. Paris, 1986.

Spiritualité et Liberation en Afrique. Paris, 1987.

ARTICLES

"Black African Arts as Cosmic Liturgy and Religious Language," *African Theology En Route.* Edited by Kofi Appiah-Kubi and Sergio Torres. Maryknoll, N.Y.: Orbis Books, 1979, pp. 137-142.

"Third World Theology—What Theology? What Third World?" *Irruption of the Third World: Challenge to Theology.* Edited by Virginia Fabella and Sergio Torres. Maryknoll, N.Y.: Orbis Books, 1983, pp. 217-222.

"An African Experience," *China Notes,* Vol. 24, Nos. 2 and 3, Spring and Summer 1986, pp. 397-398.

CHARLES NYAMITI

It is important to observe that we are here confronted with one of the chief differerences between political theologies of liberation and the thinking of Messiah's Ancestorship. The former insist on liberation of the oppressed from socio-economic ills as the principal task of the Christian; whereas our christology emphasizes liberation from sin through the life of habitual grace as the primary and indispensable ground of any Christian activity....To put political or economic liberation on a higher and more important level than that of deliverance from sin through habitual grace is to falsify the hierarchy of values in Christian conduct (Christ as Our Ancestor, p. 89).

Charles Nyamiti is an orthodox Roman Catholic theologian of liberation who believes that Christianity must be thoroughly indigenous to African culture without compromising the centrality of the teachings of the church's magisterium.

Charles Nyamiti was born in Ndala-Tabora, Tanzania, in 1931. He was reared in a devout Catholic family and received regular religious instruction in traditional Catholic teaching, both at home and in primary and secondary schools, from his parents, catechists, and missionaries. He studied at Louvain and received his Ph.D. in theology from the University of Vienna. His combination of theological, anthropological, and musical studies in Europe broadened his religious outlook and played an important role in expanding his appreciation of his own African background and culture.

After his ordination, Nyamiti served as professor of systematic theology at the seminary in Kipalapala (1967-1981) as well as parish priest (1978-1984). Since 1984 he has been professor of theology and head of the department of dogmatic theology in the Catholic Higher Institute of Eastern Africa in Nairobi, Kenya. In his move from Europe back to Africa, he began to sense the need for the creation of an indigenous African theology, one that was sufficiently flexible to repond to the rich diversity of Africa's cultural heritage. But his strongly orthodox Catholic faith, coupled with the rigorous philosophical training he had received in Europe, helped him realize that "not all of the past is to be discarded, and that not all that is new is good." His goal thus is to maintain a balance between his loyalty to church teaching and his strong grounding in African beliefs and customs.

Nyamiti's orthodox faith has made him highly critical of any form of liberation theology that does not directly and explicitly connect human oppression in all of its dimensions with its root cause, which is sin or alienation from God. For example, Nyamiti can be sympathetic to South African black theologians for their concentration on racism as a demonic form of oppression. These theologians are not "a bunch of way-out radicals," as he hears critics say. Yet, at the same time, he warns these theologians against "reducing black theology to the theme of liberation from white segregation," and he cautions his South African colleagues against fomenting a militancy which only leads to a "lack of objectivity and a distortion of the facts." A narrow provincialism that over-stresses *any* single aspect of human oppression, e.g., racism, can only lead to a diminution of concern for other significant kinds of oppression and—even worse—a failure to root racism in sin against God.

Nyamiti also faults some liberation theologians for pretending that their way is the only viable theological option for today. Such elitism only prevents these theologians from appropriating the fertile contributions being made by other church theologians. To avoid such short-sightedness, Nyamiti affirms the importance of speculation and metaphysics as important tasks for all theologians. Nyamiti understands the primary goal of theology to be the quest for the meaning of the Christian mysteries in themselves and, secondarily, to discover their implications for our lives.

In his article "Approaches to African Theology," Charles Nyamiti distinguishes among three types of African theology: 1) The speculative with its dominant concern for systematization; 2) the socio-biblical school with its grounding in the Bible and its distrust of metaphysics; 3) the militant school, found particularly in South Africa, with its focus on liberation of black people from their white oppressors. Nyamiti sees value in all three approaches. But he believes that the first two models have, until recent times, been too influenced by Western categories, failing to take into account African culture. In this lies Nyamiti's connection with liberation theology. He believes that the contextualization of African theology comes as a mandate from Vatican II, which encouraged indigenization, a necessary component of the church and its opening to the modern world. Not only must Christianity aggressively incorporate African themes and values, but simultaneously it must also come to terms with "negative factors like magic, polygamy, superstition, poverty, ignorance and disease."

One important African theme that should be incorporated into African versions of Christianity is the belief in communication with ancestors. Nyamiti contends that there is a close correlation between Catholic teaching about the intercession of the saints and the African conviction that one can communicate with one's ancestors. Christ's own ancestorship can be linked with the First Adam and thereby with every human being. Nyamiti asserts: "There are enough similarities between Christ's brother relationship to men and that of the African brother ancestor to show us that the two types of relationship have the same fundamental structure" (*Christ as Our Ancestor*, p. 23). Even the celebration of the Mass can be considered an ancestral ritual in which the Christ-ancestor comes to his people.

Marxism plays no role in Nyamiti's theological concerns, except that it has helped him realize more clearly that it is a *human* as well as a Christian duty to change the world and those social structures which sanction oppression. This is another feature of his thinking that allies him with liberation theology. For Nyamiti, theology can never be sheer speculation and contemplation. Theology by its very nature must include action, an involvement in changing the world. But, apart from this Marxist insight, Nyamiti considers Marxism an alien ideology that falsifies the Christian faith.

In brief, then, Charles Nyamiti opts for the kind of liberation theology that has its feet in two camps: the orthodox teachings of the Catholic church and the cultural setting of African societies. But Nyamiti adds that liberation theology is not the only viable theological option for today. Nor should it exclude metaphysics or confine its attention to overcoming socio-economic oppression. He agrees that liberation theology is correct in trying to rid the Christian faith of its Western bias as it struggles against all forms of oppression.

BOOKS

Christ as Our Ancestor: Christology from an African Perspective. Gwere, Zambia: Mambo Press, 1984.

Christology from Some African Perspectives (in preparation).

Introduction to African Theology (in preparation).

ARTICLES

"Approaches to African Theology." *The Emergent Gospel.* Edited by Sergio Torres and Virginia Fabella. Maryknoll, N.Y.: Orbis Books, 1978, pp. 31-46.

"Ancestral Kinship in the Trinity," *FICU,* 1987.

MERCY AMBA ODUYOYE

*Third world theology needs no other qualifying term ex-
cept that it is theology from the underside of history, and
African theology is nothing less than the insights that
Christians in Africa are bringing to Christian theology.
The challenge to theology may be specific to Africa in the
details of the confrontation, but they are part of the challenges of our human realities as a whole. To treat them as
exotic additions would be to sin against the Holy Spirit,
and that would be heresy. We have to do theology, believing that when our honest labors are offered to God,
God's holiness burns away the dross and allows the purity
of the gold to shine, leading those who live in darkness to
see a Great Light* (Hearing and Knowing, p. 76).

Mercy Amba Oduyoye has made her mark as a Third World liberation theologian in two major ways: first, as an African who envisions a theology that can be authentically both African and Christian: "being in Christ but living in Nigeria" (p. 75); and second, as an African woman who seeks to liberate the human community from entrenched structures and attitudes that perpetuate the sin of sexism. Oduyoye's understanding of the term *Third World* does not single out any particular geographical area, but, rather, refers to oppression, poverty, and inhumanity wherever they may be found. Thus, "all who do theology from the context of injustice and unrighteousness—feminists, for example—find themselves at home among Third World theologians" (p. 2).

Mercy Amba Oduyoye was born in Asamankese, Ghana, in 1934. Her father was a Methodist clergyman who served as a pastor in Ghana for 37 years, ending his career as president of the Ghana Methodist Conference. As the daughter of a pastor who served parishes in several predominantly Akan rural communities, Oduyoye received an early and extensive exposure to Akan culture. During her early years she showed no particular interest in studying theology. Her chief academic interests were geography, economics, and British history.

The final stage of her pre-secondary schooling was in a Methodist school in Mmofraturo, Kumasi, which was ahead of its time in its willingness to incorporate the contributions of Akan culture as a part of the curriculum. She received her secondary education at Achimota, Accra, where she learned the native Ga language and absorbed a high degree of Ghanian culture. The school at Achimota was co-educational and encouraged both the boys and girls to study the subjects and follow the vocations of their choice. Thus, from an early age Mercy Oduyoye was actively encouraged to revere her own cultural background and to follow her highest ambitions.

To be sure, she suffered discrimination both as an African and as a woman. Looking back, she recalls: "When I was growing up in the 1940s and the 1950s with missionaries, I did not see the missionaries' 'capacity to live in fellowship with others' unless the 'others' meant Europeans. If anything, the isolation of the missionaries from the people was more noticeable even than that of British administratrors" (p. 33). As a woman she experienced discrimination just as much in her own Akan culture as she did in her "Western Christian" influences. "With African culture, Islamic norms, Western civilization, and the church's traditional anti-feminism piled upon the African woman, the world has been led to see African women as not more than the quintessence of the status called: 'the oppressed'" (Christian Feminism and African Culture: The "Hearth" of the Matter, p. 3).

Oduyoye attended the University of Kumasi, receiving a post-secondary certificate of education in 1954. After teaching at a Methodist girl's middle school in Kumasi for several years, she continued her undergraduate education at the University of Ghana, where one of her professors, Noel Quintin King, encouraged her to study for a B.A. in religion, which she received in 1963. At the university her professors represented several Christian denominations and African backgrounds, and this deepened her appreciation for religious and cultural diversity. Oduyoye continued her education in England where she studied theology at Cambridge University with Professors Maurice Wiles, Alex Vidler, Stephen Sykes, and Basil Hall. She received a B.A. in theology from Cambridge in 1965.

Oduyoye returned to Ghana and, after serving another stint as a high school teacher, moved to Geneva. From 1967 to 1973, she was Youth Education Secretary for the World Council of Churches, a position that broadened her ecumenical interests. From 1974 to 1986, she taught in the Department of Religious Studies at the University of Ibadan in Nigeria. After serving as Henry Luce Visiting Professor at Union Theological Seminary for a year, in 1987 she assumed the position of Deputy General Secretary of the World Council of Churches, with particular responsibility for education and renewal. Oduyoye is a member of the WCC Commission on Faith and Order and both the first woman and the first African to serve as president of the World Student Christian Federation.

Oduyoye's extensive participation in the ecumenical work of the Christian churches has given her an important platform for pursuing her concerns as an African feminist. She admits that her participation in numerous conferences on both African and women's issues has stimulated her own work in both of these areas while at the same time nurturing her role as a Methodist lay preacher. She considers her own special mission to be "to call attention to missiology and to African women's potential for contributing to the theological enterprise." Since the African heritage has, for the most part, been communicated orally rather than in writing, the collection and preservation of this oral tradition is an indispensable task for African theologians. For Oduyoye, "hearing and knowing" are the seedbeds for African religion.

Oduyoye stresses how important it is for today's theologian to keep one foot in the theological enterprise and the other foot in the life of the church. "My own commitment has not only been to excellence of theological articulation in the context of the academy; it has also been to the church's life and mission. The Word of God is in the realities of everyday events. For me therefore much of doing theology is in listening to what the Spirit is saying to the churches—those who have ears can hear, reflect, tell and act as if they are really committed to the Christ way."

African theologians have a further responsibility to reinterpret Christian doctrines and sacraments in the African cultural context. For example, baptism should not be thought of as a washing away of African language and customs, as earlier Western missionaries believed. Rather, baptism is the means to reconcile and fuse the community of the African family with the community of the church in such a way that the individual can feel at home in both. Likewise the eucharist must be seen as a sacrificial feast that, with Christ, celebrates victory over exploitation and oppression. Like Geevarghese Mar Osthathios, Oduyoye considers the doctrine of the Trinity an essential model for the individual's role in the Christian community, one in which individuals, separate yet equal, are united in love.

Oduyoye has never been attracted to Marxism except insofar as it helps to pinpoint the sources of economic oppression. She asserts that it is a complete distortion of liberation theology to suggest, as some critics do, that "it is inspired by Marxism and promoted by communists."

Oduyoye has increasingly called attention to women's issues. She has not hesitated to criticize some Third World liberation theologians for their sexism. She points out: "There have been several international meetings at which Third World representatives have said that antisexism is not their priority. At times they have even said that it is not an issue in their world, where men and women *know their place* and *play their role* ungrudgingly and no one feels suffocated by society's definition of femininity and masculinity....The fact is that sexism is part of the intricate web of oppression in which most of us live, and that having attuned ourselves to it does not make it any less a factor of oppression" (Reflections from a Third World Woman's Perspective...," p.

249). What Oduyoye envisions is a genuine community—and here she evokes the Trinity—of sharing responsibility and power. Feminism has much to offer to this community, for feminism means "openness, creativity and dynamic human relationships....It seeks to express what is not so obvious, that is, that male-humanity is a partner with female-humanity, and that both expressions of humanity are needed to shape a balanced community within which each will experience a fullness of Be-ing. Feminism calls for the incorporation of the woman into the community of interpretation of what it means to be human" (*Hearing and Knowing*, p. 121).

In short, Mercy Oduyoye advocates an expanding theology of liberation that will transcend nation, class, race, and sex. "Knowing ourselves, having a sense of history, believing in the future, and the transformation brought about by the cooperation of the divine and the human in Jesus the Christ, we are (I am) freed to take part in the building up of theologies that will contribute to the transformation needed in the church and in society" (*Hearing and Knowing*, p. 149).

BOOKS

Youth Without Jobs. Ibadan: Daystar Press, 1972.

Christian Youth Work. Ibadan: Daystar Press, 1979.

And Women: Where Do They Come In? Lagos: Methodist Litertature Department, 1980.

The State of Christian Theology in Nigeria 1980/81 Edited by Oduyoye. Ibadan: Daystar Press, 1986.

Hearing and Knowing: Theological Reflections on Christianity in Africa. Maryknoll, N.Y.: Orbis Books, 1986.

ARTICLES

"Church Women and the Church's Mission in Contemporary Times: A Study of Sacrifice in Mission," *Bulletin of African Theology*, Vol. 6, No. 12, pp. 259-272.

"Naming the Woman: The Words of the Bible and the Words of the Akan," *Bulletin of African Theology*, Vol. 3, No. 5.

"The Value of African Religious Beliefs and Practices for Christian Theology," *African Theology En Route*. Edited by Kofi Appiah-Kubi and Sergio Torres. Maryknoll, N.Y.: Orbis Books, 1979, pp. 109-117.

"Reflections from a Third World Woman's Perspective: Women's Experience and Liberation Theologies," *Irruption of the Third World: Challenge to Theology*. Edited by Virginia Fabella and Sergio Torres. Maryknoll, N.Y.: Orbis Books, 1983, pp. 246-256.

"Christian Feminism and African Culture: The 'Hearth' of the Matter," unpublished, presented to Union Theological Seminary, February 1987.

"The African Family as a Symbol of Ecumenism," unpublished.

AYLWARD SHORTER

There is no reason why there should not be a plurality of African approaches to Christian theology, corresponding to a plurality of African traditional theologies....a methodology which treats African systems as a single, unified phenomenon is simply not faithful to the facts (African Christian Theology, *p. 27*).

Aylward Shorter has made his primary contribution to liberation theology in the area of cultural liberation. As a result of Western dependency, education, and modernization, Africans often feel alienated from their own native cultures. Shorter believes it essential to "de-Westernize" Africa and make Africans proud of their own rich heritage. This process will inevitably include an Africanization of the Christian faith. To be sure, socio-economic liberation is important, but Shorter's major interest is in cultural liberation.

Aylward Shorter was born in London in 1932. During his years as a student at the Downside School (a Benedictine school) from 1945 to 1950, he was exposed on a regular basis to liturgy and prayer. These became a vital part of his life and provided a spiritual underpinning to his later conviction that theology and spirituality must always go hand in hand. "Theology," he would later maintain, "should be spiritual theology. That is to say, it should not be merely speculative, but should encourage active commitment" (*African Christian Spirituality*, p. 5).

Shorter received his B.A. and M.A. degrees in modern history from Oxford. He served in the British army in Kenya and Malaysia where he first encountered the problems of communicating the Christian faith to a people of a different culture. It was also during his years of army service abroad that he experienced a religious conversion, which quickened his interest in the priesthood. He was ordained a priest in 1962, and his first assignment was to study missiology in Rome. This fortuitously happened to be the time of the first session of the Second Vatican Council. Being "in the wings" of the Council, he would later say, helped him to develop a mentality of reformation and renewal in adapting theology to a multi-cultural church. Later as a missionary priest conducting fieldwork in Ukimbu, Tanzania, Shorter immersed himself in Kimbu culture and the religious life of the native people. He did further study at Oxford, receiving a diploma in social anthropology and a D. Phil. in 1968. His doctoral thesis was a sociological study of the Kimbus of Tanzania.

Shorter served as lecturer in African pastoral anthropology at the Pastoral Institute for Eastern Africa in Gaba, Uganda, from 1968 to 1977; lecturer in social anthropology at Kipalapala Senior Seminary in Tanzania from 1977 to 1980; and professor of social anthropology at the Catholic Higher Institute of Eastern Africa in Nairobi from 1984 to 1987. A year's stint in 1982-83 at a slum parish in Nairobi opened his eyes to social justice issues and how they must be connected with the spiritual life of the religious community. In 1987 Shorter became President of the Missionary Institute in London, a theological consortium of seven Roman Catholic missionary congregations, which is affiliated with the Catholic University of Louvain, Belgium.

The decade that Shorter spent at the Gaba Pastoral Institute gave him the direct opportunity to participate in the renewal of the Catholic church in Eastern Africa and to meet Christian leaders from many African countries. And a year spent teaching in Bristol, England, reintroduced him to the writings of John Henry Newman. These writings helped him solve, to his own satisfaction, the problem of cultural relativism by appreciating faith, not as a propositional concept, but as a creative, imaginative act, what Newman himself termed "first order language."

Shorter's experience as a priest and teacher in Africa has brought him to the realization that the most important issue facing theology today is that of inculturation. Although he does not wish to downplay the socio-economic issues facing the African poor, he does fault South African liberation theologians for making blackness their number one priority. Granted, the "white Jesus" was idolatrous; but is the "black Jesus" any less so? Is diminished, oppressed humanity exclusively black? Shorter sees as a real danger how praxis focusing on blackness could become a new kind of Pelagianism.

Shorter believes that a concentration on cultural liberation raises crucial theological questions for African Christians. Jesus Christ, he says, must be understood as the Eternal Logos at the very heart of traditional culture and that this process of inculturation must be seen as evidence of the mysterious workings of the one God. But the toughest questions of all that are facing the Catholic church in Africa today are ecclesiological, namely, the importance of accepting and even encouraging a multicultural church in all its diversity, while at the same time preserving the sense of one worldwide communion. In his book, *African Christian Theology*, Shorter addresses these problems: "The church needs the African theological contribution for her own theological health. This contribution is not going to destroy or alter the universal tradition, but it may operate first of all as a corrective in a number of ways. First, it may awaken themes in universal Christianity which are dormant, or latent. Secondly, it may help to show that certain elements presented to Africa as essential in the universal tradition are in fact secondary elements, deriving from the particular Western cultural tradition" (p. 31).

Shorter is sceptical of generalists—in particular, scholars from the West—who lump together African religion as though it can all be tied up into one coherent system. But, with more than eight hundred African tribes to be studied, "We shall obviously have to wait a long time for the needed...African scholars to make their appearance." African religious pluralism is a fact that must not be ignored. "It is clear that in a pluralistic world a homogeneous religious system that is trying to swallow up other systems is out of place. What is required is a differentiated system which is in real contact through religious dialogue with other systems of belief and values in the various localities. A universal church, therefore, must be prepared to admit cultural pluralism" (p. 142).

Marxism as an ideology has no part in Shorter's theology. He has, however, come to appreciate Marxist social analysis and the problems caused by poor nations being forced to depend on the rich nations. Shorter believes that most African theologians espouse the dependency theory, but all of them strongly reject Marxism as an atheistic ideology. Thus, Shorter—like so many Third World liberation theologians—believes it quite proper to utilize Marxist social analysis without succumbing to Marxist ideology.

Aylward Shorter's scholarly contributions have been described by the English theologian Adrian Hastings as "watering the roots of African theology." Shorter accepts this characterization. And he hopes to stimulate other African theologians to make African cultural and religious pluralism better known in North America. He sees his own role as twofold: to "water the roots" of an indigenous African theology for the Africans themselves, and to make known these insights to the Western world. "I hope that my work," he says, "represents an instance of the mutual enrichment between local churches, spoken of by Paul VI in *Evangelii Nuntiandi*, 63."

BOOKS

Chiefship in Western Tanzania. Oxford: Clarendon, 1972.

African Culture and the Christian Church. London: Chapman, 1973.

African Christian Theology: Adaptation or Incarnation? Maryknoll, N.Y.: Orbis Books, 1977.

Priest in the Village. London: Chapman, 1979.

African Christian Spirituality. Maryknoll, N.Y.: Orbis Books, 1980.

Revelation and its Interpretation. London: Chapman, 1983.

Jesus and the Witchdoctor. London: Chapman, 1985.

ARTICLES

"African Traditional Religion: Its Relevance in the Contemporary World," *Cross Currents*, Vol. 28, no. 4, 1978-9, pp. 421-431.

"Creative Imagination and the Language of Religious Traditions in Africa," *Kerygma*, 35, Vol. 14, 1980, pp. 175-204.

"Christian Healing and Traditional Medicine in Africa," *Kerygma*, 46, Vol. 20, 1986, pp. 51-58.

DESMOND TUTU

If anyone were to show me that apartheid is biblical or Christian, I have said before, and I reiterate now, that I would burn my Bible and cease to be Christian. I will want to show that the Christian Bible and the Gospel of Jesus Christ Our Lord is subversive of all injustice and evil, oppression and exploitation, and that God is on the side of the oppressed and the downtrodden, that He is the liberator God of the Exodus, who leads His people out of every kind of bondage, spiritual, political, social and economic, and nothing will thwart Him from achieving the goal of the liberation of all His people and the whole of His creation (Hope and Suffering, *pp. 155-156).*

64

Winner of the Nobel Peace Prize in 1984, Desmond Tutu has become known throughout the world for his vigorous Christian witness in the nonviolent struggle for liberation from the evils of apartheid in his native country of South Africa. The apartheid system, which keeps blacks in an inferior position to whites, is for Tutu completely contradictory to the demands of the Christian gospel. Tutu has dedicated his life to overcoming the evils of apartheid, even going so far as to predict that there will be a black prime minister in South Africa by the early 1990s.

Desmond Tutu was born in 1931 in Klerksdorp, a town west of Johannesburg in Western Transvaal. His father belonged to the Methodist Church and taught in a primary school. Tutu attended a boarding school at Roodeport, which was run by a Swedish Lutheran mission. When he was fourteen, Tutu contracted tuberculosis and was hospitalized for almost two years in Sophiatown, a hospital supervised by the Catholic Community of the Resurrection.

It was during this hospital stay that Tutu came under the influence of the Anglican priest, Trevor Huddleston, who at the time was a priest in the black suburb of Johannesburg. Tutu recalls that he first met Trevor Huddleston when he was only 8 or 9 years of age. Tutu's mother worked as a domestic cook in a hostel for blind black women. Huddleston walked by the two of them one day and doffed his hat to Tutu's mother. This one experience had a profound effect upon the young Tutu. He realized that there were some white people who had respect for blacks.

Although originally he had hoped to become a physician, Tutu's family could not afford to send him to medical school. Instead he earned a teacher's certificate at the Pretoria Bantu Normal College in 1953, and a year later received a B.A. degree from the University of South Africa. For the next three years he taught high school and during this period he decided to study for the ministry. From 1958 to 1960 he was a seminary student at St. Peter's Theological College in Johannesburg. He was ordained a deacon in the Episcopal church in 1960 and a year later he became a priest.

In 1962 Desmond Tutu traveled to England where he lived for the next five years. He received B.D. and M.Th. degrees in theology at King's College, London, and during that period served as a curate at St. Alban's. In the late 1960s, he returned home where he served on the faculty of the Federated Theological Seminary in Alice Cape, as well as in the department of theology at the University of Botswana. He also managed to wear a third hat as chaplain at the University of Fort Hare. Once again England beckoned, and in the early 1970s Tutu served a three-year stint as Associate Director of the Theological Education Fund of the World Council of Churches, headquartered in Bromley, Kent.

In 1975 Tutu was appointed Dean of the cathedral at Johannesburg, the first black person to hold that post. A year later he became Bishop of Lesotho and soon thereafter became General Secretary of the South African Council of Churches. Tutu continued to climb the ecclesiastical ladder; he was elected Bishop of Johannesburg in 1985 and only a year later he was appointed Archbishop of Cape Town. In 1987 at the Fifth General Assembly of the All Africa Conference of Churches meeting in Lome, Tutu was elected to the presidency of this continent-wide ecumenical organization.

Desmond Tutu has been awarded more than twenty honorary doctorates and numerous other awards, including the Nobel Peace Prize. The citation of the Norwegian Nobel Committee reads:

> The committee has attached importance to Desmond Tutu's role as a unifying leader figure in the campaign to resolve the problems of apartheid in South Africa....Through the award of this year's Peace Prize, the committee wishes to direct attention to the nonviolent struggle for liberation to which Desmond Tutu belongs, a struggle in which black and white South Africans unite to bring their country out of conflict and crisis.

Desmond Tutu's life and ministry incarnate the main features of Third World liberation theology. In his vigorous espousal of liberation he has not hesitated to speak his mind to both whites and blacks. To whites he has issued the challenge: "Join in the liberation struggle. Throw off your lethargy, and the apathy of affluence. Work for a better South Africa for yourselves, ourselves, and for our children" (*Crying in the Wilderness*, pp. 43-44). To his own black people he testifies: "For those among our peoples who feel despondent and hopeless, I want to assert that we shall be free. Do not despair of this. We shall be free because our cause is a just cause....Let us rejoice. Let us lift up our heads and straighten our drooping shoulders. God cares and God will act decisively to bring justice, peace and reconciliation in our land" (p. 89).

In his speeches and writings Desmond Tutu has all the earmarks of a liberation theologian. He disavows the kind of Western theology that wafts from professorial studies and instead affirms the need for a theology that will emerge from "the anvil of adversity in the heat of battle." He talks of a God of "the poor, hungry and naked" who is on the side of "the oppressed, the marginalized and the exploited." This God is the God of the Bible, the God of Moses leading his people out of oppression to the promised land, and the God of Jesus whose resurrection marks the culmination of the liberation of humanity from the realm of darkness into the light of the Kingdom.

For Tutu, theology must evolve from the particular historical situation in South Africa. Indeed there must be a plurality of theologies since human apprehension of the transcendent has its roots in distinctive historical contexts. However, in the past, indigenization has been only feeble, failing to include the cutting edge of social, political and economic realities. For some Africans— including some African theologians—the kind of black theology now emerging from South Africa may seem abrasive and too focused on the apartheid system. But, says Tutu, this abrasiveness may have a few lessons for the kind of African theology that puts indigenization ahead of economic, social, and racial liberation. If black theology is to be faulted for its abrasiveness, then the African theology that stresses cultural liberation can be criticized for lacking a prophetic mission to liberate the black oppressed from their oppressor. Tutu is also a vigorous advocate of women's liberation, including women's ordination, in the Anglican communion, declaring: "Women, we need you to give us back our faith in humanity." He also believes that in the past Christians have made too much of "the Fatherhood of God" and now need to refer more to "the Motherhood of God" (*Crying in the Wilderness*, p. 120).

Tutu firmly believes that there should be a radical redistribution of wealth and a more equitable distribution of the resources of the land in South Africa. He urges South African whites to agree voluntarily to a lower standard of living and to accept political power-sharing in an orderly transfer of power. The alternative will be bloodshed and chaos (*Crying in the Wilderness*, p. 44). But in putting forth these ideas Tutu makes no use of Marxism. "An ideology that denies that men and women are created in the image of God is incompatible with Christianity." His convictions are grounded in his devout Christian faith. He believes that all people are children of God—and that what blacks want for themselves is exactly what whites want for themselves, no more, no less.

Desmond Tutu is the apostle of hope in a despairing world, a modern-day prophet who remains convinced—solely because of his Christian faith—that blacks and whites can live together if they are willing to denounce all that is contrary to God's love that has been revealed for every person in the life of Jesus Christ. God's love is constant and infinite. What we need most of all is "to be liberated from ourselves....We are liberated according to our capacity to love. Until we see God in every person and respond in love, we will not be free."

BOOKS

Crying in the Wilderness: The Struggle for Justice in South Africa. Grand Rapids, Michigan: Wm. B. Eerdmans, 1982.

Hope and Suffering: Sermons and Speeches. Grand Rapids, Michigan: Wm. B. Eerdmans, 1983.

ARTICLES

"Black Theology/African Theology—Soul Mates or Antagonists?" *Journal of Religious Thought*, Vol. 32, No. 2 (Fall-Winter 1975), pp. 25-33.

"Whither African Theology?" *Christianity in Independent Africa.* Edited by Edward Fashole-Luke. London: Rex Collings, 1978, pp. 364-370.

PART II

ASIA

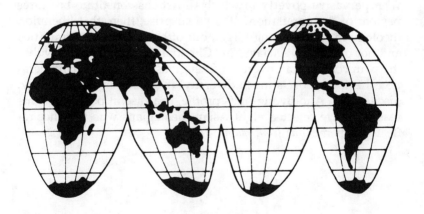

The ingredient that gives Asian liberation theology its distinctive flavor is Christianity's status as a minority religion in a continent in which Hinduism and Buddhism are the major faiths. Here positive interfaith dialogue becomes an essential imperative for liberation theology. It is, therefore, incumbent upon the Christian faith to shed its traditional exclusivism and become an equal partner in the ongoing dialogue with other religions. As Tissa Balasuriya puts it: "It is my conviction that a profound change in Christian theology is necessary if the message of Christ is to be meaningful for Asia and Asians. This will mean a reconversion of all Christians to the core of the gospel" (*Planetary Theology*, p. 139).

Having acknowledged this point, however, one should also be aware of the tremendous poverty that exists in Asia today. To quote Balasuriya again: "Asia, with 85 to 90 percent of the world's poor, is a continent of large and growing populations. Over 40 percent of all Asians are below fifteen years of age and only five percent above sixty years" (p. 55).

Thus, the basic problem that Asian liberation theologians confront is: How do we sing the Lord's song on a continent teeming with pervasive poverty in which Christians constitute but three percent of the population? It is no surprise, then, that liberation theology in Asia is being forged out of base *human* communities and not out of tiny enclaves of "Christians only." Yet even within the twin contexts of poverty and religious pluralism Asian liberation theology reflects much diversity. (Korean minjung theology, discussed in Ahn Byung-mu's profile, is a case in point.) For this reason I have selected eight Asian theologians who together reflect the theme: *one from many.*

CARLOS H. ABESAMIS

Asian theology, aiming to respond to the imperative put to it by Asian reality, has two basic characteristics: its "Third-Worldness" (with its thrust toward socio-political and total human liberation of the poor, the deprived, and the oppressed) and its "Asianness" (the peculiar Asian character, whatever that happens to be in our different situations respectively). Both of these characteristics are essential to today's theology and are inseparable, one from the other (Faith and Life Reflections from the Grassroots in the Philippines, *p. 134*).

Carlos Abesamis believes that the real theologians are the grassroots poor who are seeking to break out of the chains of oppression and silence. He sees his role as that of a technician who offers his expertise in the Bible as a means of helping the poor interpret their plight from a Christian perspective.

Carlos Abesamis was born in Naga in the Philippines in 1934. From his earliest years he was imbued with a strong social conscience. He still recalls that when he was only five years old his father told him: "The house help should eat the same food as we." In many homes at that time the pet dogs and cats ate better than did the house boys and house maids.

Abesamis received a licentiate in sacred theology from the University of Innsbruck, Austria, where he studied under the eminent Catholic theologian, Karl Rahner. During this period he was ordained a Jesuit priest. He did further study at the Pontifical Institute in Rome where he received a licentiate in Sacred Scripture. He has been a professor of New Testament at the Loyola School of Theology in the Philippines since 1968; since 1974 he has served as theologian for the National Catholic Bishops' Secretariat for Social Action, Justice, and Peace, in Manila.

Although he recalls no earth-shaking experiences that shaped his present theological views, during his seminary days he found himself growing increasingly sensitive to issues directly related to poverty. He became more and more dissatisfied with the comfortable life-style of the seminary professors and students, which seemed so alien to the poverty of the people they were being trained to serve. After becoming a professor of biblical studies in the Philippines, Abesamis took up tasks which nurtured his social conscience. During the summer months, he would serve as a priest in the villages of the rural areas near Manila. One particular summer he joined a group of priests in starting an experimental Third World seminary. Living and working as a community, committed to the poor and oppressed, the priests themselves worked side-by-side with the sugar plantation laborers. These "immersions," he recalls, strengthened his contact with the realities of the soil and its people.

Gradually through his biblical studies and his involvement in the life of the poor he began to understand the Bible in a new light. "The eyeglasses I have used are Third World glasses which are an apt instrument for discovering meanings faithful to the original context and relevant to our Third World context. This endeavor, of course, yields a liberating Bible and a liberating spirituality and praxis." Abesamis does not consider himself a liberation theologian but rather a student of the Bible who has discovered the core message of the Bible to be a liberating praxis.

Through "rediscovering the Bible" Abesamis advocates a model for "doing theology" that flows from the Christian base communities and which, he believes, has a fourfold emphasis: 1) It is based on the contemporary life-situation and history of the poor and oppressed. 2) It goes through a process of careful scientific analysis. 3) It is grounded in the light of a biblico-historical faith, further infused with the wisdom of native religion. 4) It issues in the kind of action that transforms the individual and society.

According to Abesamis his major contribution to theology is the third step, i.e., a deepened understanding of and appreciation for the insights of the biblico-historical faith. To that end he devotes much of his time working in partnership with the base communities, holding seminars and workshops, serving as a midwife to this theology-from-below in its birthing stages. He says that a major impediment to his work is the heavy weight of tradition, which is fraught with medieval and colonial baggage that many seminary professors, church authorities, and even ordinary church folk still carry around in cerebral fashion. He has discovered that the best way to break through the head into the heart is a pastoral approach, confronting directly the problems and pains of the oppressed as they experience them first-hand in their daily lives. He says: "If theology is to be done at all, the authors of such a theology would have to be the grassroots people themselves, or, at least, people who by origin or social position may not be grassroots but who are making efforts to remold their minds and hearts to see reality from the standpoint of the liberated grassroots poor" ("Faith and Life Reflections from the Grassroots in the Philippines," p. 138). If theology cannot be done this way by "non-grassroots people," then it is better for them to remain silent.

Abesamis's use of Marxism has been only tangential and indirect. He does believe that the Marxist critique of capitalism is valid and is therefore a useful instrument for theologians who deal directly with contemporary social realities. But to admit this does not thereby make him a Marxist. He asks: Why can't one use some of the insights of Marx as one does the insights of other thinkers without being branded a Marxist?

Abesamis has undergone a complete change in his thinking

with respect to the United States. He originally considered the United States the "great liberator." But in the 1960s and 1970s, he became aware of what he calls the "baneful activities" of the transnational corporations controlled by business interests in the United States, and of the influence of the United States military forces on Philippine soil. He now blames the USA for much of the destruction and barbarism that President Ferdinand Marcos let loose on his own people. It is his dream that liberation theology can fire North Americans with missionary zeal designed to force the Central Intelligence Agency out of the Philippines. He believes that the Filipinos themselves can eventually take care of the transnational companies, but the CIA is too powerful and clandestine to be eliminated without assistance from the Americans themselves. He declares: "In the Philippines, we currently live our days and nights in the uncomfortable embrace of the CIA's Low Intensity Conflict. In this scheme, a Filipino must kill a brother Filipino in order to fulfill the Pentagon dream of military bases and economic empires firmly planted on our soil."

Abesamis's strong anti-American stand has not come from Marxism nor communist insurgence in the Philippines. He insists that it has come from his own immersion in the grassroots communities of the poor who suffer from American imperialism. Abesamis is also highly critical of fundamentalist Protestant missionaries, mostly imports from the United States, who preach a message of personal salvation that only serves to divert the Filipino poor from confronting their serious problems of oppression and suffering. These fundamentalist missionaries encourage passive acceptance of the social and economic status quo in order to gain glory in the life-to-come. Such religion, Abesamis claims, only plays into the hands of the oppressors and makes the liberation of the oppressed that much more difficult.

In his ministry, Carlos Abesamis is trying to weave the thread of a liberating faith into the very fabric of the lives of the poor people of the Philippines, a faith which for Abesamis must find its roots in the biblical message of love and justice for all people.

BOOKS

Where Are We Going: Heaven or New World? Manila: Communications Foundation of Asia, 1983.

Exploring the Core of Biblical Faith. Quezon City: Claretian Publications, 1986.

The Mission of Jesus and Good News to the Poor. Quezon City, Philippines: Claretian Publications, 1987.

ARTICLES

"Faith and Life Reflections from the Grassroots in the Philippines," *Asia's Struggle for Full Humanity: Towards a Relevant Theology.* Edited by Virginia Fabella. Maryknoll, N.Y.: Orbis Books, 1980, pp. 123-140.

"The Biblical Roots of Justice," *Word and World: Theology for Chrisitan Ministry,* Vol. 12, No. 1, Winter 1987, pp. 12-22.

AHN BYUNG-MU

No one can deny that Jesus was standing on the side of the poor. Jesus, most of all in his companionship with persons who were treated as sinners, with the abandoned and alienated by the establishment in that time, accepted them as children of God without any pre-conditions; he was a friend of the minjung. This understanding of Jesus...provides us with a key to understanding Jesus as the living Christ of the present, and thus to accept him as our liberator today (International Review of Mission, p. 91).

Ahn Byung-mu is a proponent of minjung theology. Minjung is a synonym for the alienated peoples of Korea. Ahn believes that minjung has a broader connotation than "those people who are poor." The minjung include women, political outcasts, the illiterate, the illegitimate, laborers—in short, all people who suffer from discrimination. From a sociological viewpoint, minjung designates a class of people who are treated as less than fully human and who are prisoners of alien social structures. Ahn believes that the liberation of the minjung is at the heart of the gospel message and that Jesus who lived two thousand years ago lives today in the midst of the minjung.

Ahn Byung-mu was born in the Pyung-ahn-nam Do Province of North Korea in 1922 when Manchuria was still under Japanese military control. After Korea achieved her independence from Japan, Ahn moved to South Korea and received a B.A. degree in sociology from Seoul National University. During this period of his life, Ahn became more and more aware of the plight of the poor and alienated peoples of Korea. At one time he attempted to establish a Christian communal life for some of these alienated people who lived near Seoul and patterned his group after the basic Christian communities in Latin America. This venture eventually failed. In 1956 Ahn matriculated to the University of Heidelberg in Germany to study theology. There he became absorbed in the study of the gospels and received his Ph.D. degree in New Testament. In 1965 he returned to his native country to become Dean of Choong-ang Seminary. From 1970 to 1987, he served as professor of theology in Han-shin University, and he also served as Dean of the Graduate School of Han-shin University from 1985 to 1987. He is Director of Korea Theological Study Institute in Seoul, an institution which he helped to establish in 1972.

Throughout his adult life, Ahn Byung-mu has been very much involved in political activism. He has been expelled twice—in 1975 and again in 1980—from the university and has been imprisoned for his political "crimes." Ahn maintains that he "found minjung" through his own life experiences and his reading of the gospels. For him the starting point of minjung theology is to be found in the recent awakening of alienated Korean Christians and their struggles for liberation from military dictatorship during the 1970s. These minjung have, on the one hand, had as their goal the democratization of their society by means of the overthrow of the military dictatorship; and, on the other hand, have sought for liberation of the outcasts from all forms of social discrimination. In their struggles—and they single out, in particular, the Kwanju massacre of 1980 in which several hundred people (some residents estimate two thousand) were killed in an insurrection against the government for imposing martial law—the minjung have come to realize that Korean military dictatorship and American imperialism are two sides of the same coin.

Minjung theology was born and has continued to grow out of theological reflection on the sufferings of the minjung. Minjung theology seeks to free itself from the Western versions of theology, insisting that the theology of the West is but another example of imperialism. Minjung theology attempts to read and understand the Bible from the vantage point of the politically, economically, and culturally alienated.

As a biblical theologian, Ahn believes that the liberation of minjung is Jesus' central affirmation. Ahn's particular specialty is the gospel of Mark. He believes that Mark's exposition of the life of Jesus is the story of Jesus relating to the minjung of his time. Ahn often speaks of the "Jesus-event" as Jesus' identification with the minjung of every age. Ahn states: "Liberation is, first of all, a concept that makes the oppressed, the poor, the suffering, its object. Accordingly, Jesus as a friend of minjung belongs to the same concept as that of Jesus, the liberator" (*International Review*, p. 90). Ahn's theology is what he calls a "theology of events." The Jesus-event is the minjung-event; the two cannot be separated. To attempt to separate Jesus from minjung—to make one the subject and the other the object—is a false Western dualism. Ahn even suggests that, for him, Jesus is not a separate individual, but a collective being who encompasses the minjung.

Another distinctive feature of Ahn's minjung theology, which ties in with his view of the Jesus-event, is his contention that minjung is the subject, not the object, of salvation. God is not a separate object. God exists as subject in the form of minjung. We are saved only when we hear the anguished cries of the suffering minjung and respond to this suffering by identifying ourselves with the minjung as Jesus did. The minjung extend their hands as savior to us. We learn about Jesus as we respond to the alienated in their suffering, their language, their stories. These stories of the minjung become the medium through which the Jesus-event is transmitted. For this very reason the Korean tradition, native religions, and indigenous myths become as sacred in transmitting the

Jesus-event as do the stories in the Bible. These stories, coming out of the lives of the Korean minjung, unmask the structures of a deeply oppressive society from which Jesus is the liberator.

Ahn believes that the original form of the Christian church consisted of eschatological communities of Jesus' minjung who gathered together in response to their conviction that Jesus would liberate them. Ahn believes that one of the chief tasks of Christians today is to recover this original form of the Christian community as one working for the transformation of church and society. Ahn sees signs of this recovery in the minjung communities of today's Korea.

Ahn further believes that at the heart of the Christian faith is the idea of public ownership and a strong resistance to private ownership. For him private monopoly of both material goods and political power is anti-God, because it is anti-minjung; it only perpetuates the oppression of the majority by the oppressor minority. And here Ahn contends that contemporary theologians must come to terms with the Marxist challenge to capitalism. Ahn notes that it is extremely dangerous in Korea these days to express any sympathy toward Marxist social analysis. Indeed there is no way in South Korea to be a professing Marxist without exposing oneself to the danger of imprisonment and even death. Still, Ahn contends that it was Karl Marx who helped open the eyes of the oppressed to the enormous unrighteousness of a capitalist society. Theologians today simply cannot adhere to the old theologies that have not come to terms with Marxist social analysis. Having said this, however, Ahn does not think that the crisis of the present world will be overcome by means of intramural debate at the ideological level. What is required is a true and open dialogue in which each tries to understand the other in seeking to free the minjung.

In recent years human rights and social justice have been Ahn's chief concerns. He has been giving increasing attention to the concept of *kong* (public ownership), materialism, and class. He believes that a combination of these three interwoven themes must be the center of future theological reflection in the present struggle on the part of the Korean minjung for democratization, liberation, and for the reunification of North and South Korea. National reunification has become a particularly urgent concern for Ahn. He is convinced that the continuing division of his country into two parts is a major cause today of the suffering of Korea's minjung, who in both the north and south, crave liberation.

It is Ahn's fervent hope that his Korean minjung theology will not be studied and dissected merely as one theological system, for minjung theology is in reality a cry of the oppressed for deliverance. It cannot make a new world, but perhaps a minjung praxis can make a difference.

BOOKS
(all in Korean)

History and Witness, 1972.

Jesus, The Liberator, 1975.

Biblical Existence, 1975.

Time and Testimony, 1978.

History and Interpretation, 1982.

Introduction to the New Testament, 1982.

With Minjung, Before God, 1986.

The Stories of Minjung Theology, 1987.

ARTICLES

"Jesus and the Minjung in the Gospel of Mark," *Minjung Theology: People as the Subjects of History.* Edited by the Commission on Theological Concerns of the Christian Conference of Asia. Maryknoll, N.Y.: Orbis Books, 1983, pp. 138-152.

"The Korean Church's Understanding of Jesus: An Historical Review," *International Review of Mission,* Vol. 74, No. 293, Jan. 1985, pp. 81-91.

"The Body of Jesus-Event Tradition," *East Asia Journal of Theology,* Vol. 3, No. 2, October 1985, pp. 293-310.

TISSA BALASURIYA

Christians now have a greater realization of the immense spiritual treasure of the great world religions. They recognize that all these religions share in some way in the truth about ultimate human destiny and happiness both here and hereafter. We have come to see better that truth can have many aspects and be understood by different peoples in different ways—even though the truth in itself is one (The Eucharist and Human Liberation, *p. 152*).

Tissa Balasuriya is above all an advocate of a planet-wide liberation theology, one that encompasses all social classes, races, genders, and religions. He warns against those indigenous forms of liberation theology that focus too much on their own parochial concerns. We are all citizens of one world and, therefore, it is incumbent on us to incorporate the shared values to be found in all societies and religions into our own beliefs, liturgies, and practices. Balasuriya writes: "It will be a happy day in our land, when without fear or scandal we Christians...join Buddhists in honoring the memory of one who really has been a light of the East" (p. 157).

Tissa Balasuriya was born in Ceylon, now Sri Lanka, in 1924. He received his B.A. in economics and political science at the University of Ceylon in 1945. His studies in these fields gave him new insights into the exploitation of the poor throughout Asia. Balasuriya traces the origins of his theology of liberation to his university years. Although during the early 1940s the University of Ceylon was a hotbed of nationalism and socialism, Balasuriya identified himself with a new challenge to social injustice led by a small group of Catholic priests. During these years the struggle for independence on the part of the Indian National Congress had a profound impact on Balasuriya, in particular, the deep spirituality so vivid in the two leaders, Mohandas Gandhi and Jawaharlal Nehru. He read their writings and autobiographies as well as the spiritual writings of Catholic mystics. He also turned his attention to recent papal encyclicals including *Rerum Novarum* and *Quadragesimo Anno*.

Balasuriya then matriculated to Rome where he lived with students from many different countries. There he began to realize the great difficulty Asians have in communicating their heritage to Europeans and North Americans. He received a degree in theology from the Gregorian University and was ordained a priest in Rome in 1952. He has been an Oblate of Mary Immaculate since 1965.

Balasuriya returned to Sri Lanka in 1953, where he became more and more convinced that the traditional Western approaches to theology were no longer compatible with rising Buddhist nationalism that was so critical of the forms of Christianity then practiced in Sri Lanka. In 1962, after serving as a priest in Sri Lanka for a decade, Balasuriya traveled to Oxford University for a postgraduate course in economics. He became so dissatisfied with the way that capitalism was extolled by the academic establishment that he dropped out and went to Paris to study at the Institut

Catholique and the Faculty of Sociology at the University of Paris. These were the days of Vatican II, and in Paris as elsewhere, it was a time of rich intellectual and spiritual ferment. Balasuriya threw himself into this new wave of freedom. Indeed, he looks back to the early 1960s as the time when he finally said goodbye to Aristotelian philosophy and Thomistic theology.

By the mid-1960s, Balasuriya's deepening concern for justice for the poor and oppressed of Asia, and a new openness to the other religions of Asia, had taken hold. From 1964 to 1971 he was rector of Aquinas University in Colombo. There he sought to incorporate the new vision of Vatican II by encouraging the church to open its windows to the modern world. But the Catholic hierarchy in Sri Lanka resisted his efforts. Equally intransigent were the powerful capitalists in Sri Lanka who showed little concern for the plight of the vast numbers of the poor and oppressed. During the decade from 1969 to 1979, Balasuriya also served as Asian Chaplain of the international movement of Catholic students, and he came to identify with these students in their social radicalism and their search for a more authentic spirituality.

In 1968 Balasuriya attended a consultation on Theology and Development sponsored by the World Council of Churches in Geneva. There he met Gustavo Gutiérrez with his *A Theology of Liberation* in mimeographed form. "We had many fruitful discussions. This seminar convinced me of our approaches and pushed them further."

Convinced that a radically new approach to theology and its relationship to social problems was desperately needed, Balasuriya resigned the rectorship of Aquinas University in 1971 and went to live in Talahena village, eight miles from Colombo. That same year he helped to found the Centre for Society and Religion in Talahena, which later moved to Colombo. This was during the same period that Sri Lanka achieved its independence from England and also during the time that Aloysius Pieris, Paul Casperz and others were establishing similar centers in Sri Lanka. Through the years Balasuriya has thrown himself into social justice issues; and today, he says, "the total crisis in Sri Lanka society is engulfing us."

Balasuriya points out that Asia contains 85 to 90 percent of the world's poor and that more than 40 percent of the world's poor are under 15 years of age. In calling attention to these distressing facts, Balasuriya chides his Latin American colleagues for assuming that their area of the world is the only one that suffers from poverty. After all, he notes, Asia contains more than half of the human race and Asians live in poverty much worse than that of the average Latin American. Balasuriya maintains that "Asians are the poor of the world. They have been exploited for thousands of years—five hundred of those years by Europeans. Asia is the continent of the hungry masses of humanity" ("The Asians," p. 259).

In his analysis of the causes of poverty, Balasuriya adds a new twist when he underscores the relationship between people and the land which is, after all, "the main resource base for living." Latin American countries such as Brazil and Argentina are rich in material resources and do not have the population density of Asian countries such as China, India, and Bangladesh. Then, too, many, if not all, Latin American countries have anti-Asian legislation in their immigration policies. Balasuriya challenges both his North American and Latin American counterparts: "Our people have no food, no land. You are the world's landlords. You control the resources that can make human life possible for our people. But do you even consider sharing them?" (p. 261).

Balasuriya insists that a fundamental restructuring of the distribution of the world's land and resources is imperative. He condemns the excesses of capitalism for perpetuating the present glaring social inequities. "We live in a capitalistic world system dominated by the western powers. By and large capitalism as a system of economic relationships based on profit maximization for private interests has been and is the principal enemy of economic development and social justice in the Third World" (*Planetary Theology*, p. 96).

Balasuriya believes that "a classless society would be preferable" (p. 46) to all other societies. But this does not mean that he has jumped on the Marxist bandwagon. While he acknowledges that "Marxism as a fact of history both in the real world and in the world of ideas is very important," he adds: "I have not accepted Marxism as an adequate interpretation of reality, nor have I rejected it totally as bad. It has contributed much to sharpening critical thinking and advancing radical social changes. It has also its limitations—in its dogmatism...and its authoritarianism in practice." Balasuriya criticizes most socialist societies today for their neglect of human rights and maintains that these societies can be and often are as inhuman in their treatment of many of their citizens as are capitalist societies. The major challenge for Asia today is not to choose between capitalism and socialism. The most urgent challenge "is human life itself—the struggle for life which is the basic issue for the vast majority of Asia's massive and growing population" (p. 134)—and that this absolutely basic problem will only begin to be solved through a more equitable re-distribution of land and resources. Such a redistribution "is more basic than issues of religion, culture, or ideology" (p. 134).

Balasuriya is also a vigorous advocate of the rights of women. He points to the incredibly unfair treatment of women throughout Asia, a condition for which the indigenous Asian religions share a large measure of responsibility. Christians should take the lead in giving women equal rights. One way to do this is to end male clerical domination. The church has been utterly wrong in putting "God on the side of the dominating male...there is no acceptance of the fundamental equality of men and women in the life of the church" ("Toward the Liberation of Theology in Asia," p. 22). What is needed, Balasuriya contends, is an entirely new orienta-tion in theology that attacks sexism as well as all the other injus-tices that exist on a planetary basis.

Another feature of Balisuriya' s theology of liberation is his suggestion that the church' s liturgy should be action-oriented, a liturgy that does not look inward to individual and church-centered concerns, but instead turns outward to issues of justice and peace—to "the efforts of a people for their self-liberation from poverty, oppression, affluence, lack of freedom, and so forth" (*The Eucharist and Human Liberation*, p. 140). It is the sacrament of the eucharist which should become the central focus for human libera-tion. It is the presence of Christ in the eucharist that challenges participants to turn their attention to everyday concerns that af-fect their lives—food, clothing, shelter, health, education, justice and religious harmony (p. 136). Heretofore there has been too much emphasis on the *ex opera operato* dimension of the euchar-ist. All of the sacraments need to be purified of their "irrelevant sentimentality and taken right into the midst of the struggle be-tween good and evil that is constantly being waged within every person and society" (pp. 137-138).

Perhaps the most important of the many contributions that Tis-sa Balasuriya is making to Third World liberation theology is his advocacy of a worldwide theology that transcends all human par-ticularities. Like Aloysius Pieris, he urges greater understanding and appreciation among the religions of East and West. In his use of such phrases as "the cosmic Christ" and "the ontological universality of Christ," Balasuriya is encouraging Christians to work toward a world religious community in which all people are loved and respected. Balasuriya believes that the major living religions of the world have an indispensable role in contributing to "an ecumenism of all religions so that there would be one common core of spirituality for the global community" (*Planetary Theology,* p. 140). Here Jesus is the perfect model for Christians. For Jesus went beyond the particularities of his own Jewish heritage just as we should go beyond the Christian particularities of our day. "The human life of Jesus of Nazareth is a supreme example for us of personal commitment to human liberation; the revelation of Jesus as the cosmic Christ gives us further insights into the evolution of the entire universe and of human history" (p. 185).

BOOKS

The Eucharist and Human Liberation. Maryknoll, N.Y.: Orbis Books, 1979.

Planetary Theology. Maryknoll, N.Y.: Orbis Books, 1984.

God Has No Favorites. Maryknoll, N.Y.: Orbis Books, 1988.

ARTICLES

"Toward the Liberation of Theology in Asia," *Asia's Struggle for Full Humanity.* Edited by Virginia Fabella. Maryknoll, N.Y.: Orbis Books, 1981, pp. 16-28.

"The Asians," *The Challenge of Basic Christian Communities.* Edited by Sergio Torres and John Eagleson. Maryknoll, N.Y.: Orbis Books, 1981, pp. 259-262.

KOSUKE KOYAMA

On my way to the country church, I never fail to see a herd of waterbuffaloes grazing in the muddy paddy field. This sight is an inspiring moment for me. Why? Because it reminds me that the people to whom I am to bring the gospel of Christ spend most of their time with these waterbuffaloes in the rice field. The waterbuffaloes tell me that I must preach to these farmers in the simplest sentence-structure and thought-development. They remind me to discard all abstract ideas and to use exclusively objects that are immediately tangible. "Sticky rice," "banana," "pepper," "dog," "cat," "bicycle," "rainy season," "leaking house," "fishing," "cock-fighting," "lotterry," "stomach-ache"—these are meaningful words for them. "This morning," I say to myself, "I will try to bring the gospel of Christ through the medium of cock-fighting" (Waterbuffalo Theology, *pp. vii-viii*).

In his experience as a missionary in Thailand, Kosuke Koyama learned first-hand what has become his most distinctive contribution to liberation theology: to indigenize the Christian faith into a "theology from below."

Kosuke Koyama was born in Tokyo, Japan, in 1929. He graduated from Tokyo Union Theological Seminary in 1952 and received his B.D. degree from Drew University in 1954. He obtained a master of theology degree from Princeton Theological Seminary in 1955 and his Ph.D. degree from Princeton in 1959. He has served as: Lecturer in Systematic Theology at Thailand Theological Seminary, Chiengmai, Thailand (1960-1968); Director of the Association of Theological Schools in South East Asia and Dean of the South East Asia Graduate School of Theology (1968-1974); Senior Lecturer in Phenomenology of Religion at the University of Otago, Dunedin, New Zealand (1974-1979). In 1980 he became Professor of Ecumenics and World Christianity at Union Theological Seminary, where, since 1983, he has been John D. Rockefeller, Jr. Professor of Ecumenics and World Christianity. Koyama was ordained to the ministry of the United Church of Christ in Thailand in 1961.

According to Koyama, two experiences had a profound impact in the shaping of his theological views. The first was living in Japan during the Second World War and seeing its defeat by the Allied powers in 1945. Baptized into "the religion of the enemy" in 1942, Koyama witnessed the devastation of Tokyo by Allied bombings. As he described it: "With my own eyes I saw Tokyo become wilderness by the constant bombings. This seeing the wilderness of Tokyo has become, over the years, a 'theological' experience...As I reflected on the destruction of Japan I was led to evaluate critically my own nature-oriented culture, focusing on emperor worship and sun worship. Out of this critique arose the intriguing challenge of the Bible" (*Mount Fuji and Mount Sinai*, p. ix).

This experience of having witnessed the destruction and defeat of his native country by a "Christian" nation left Koyama with the intense feeling of being deserted, forsaken, and betrayed. He began to realize that history is replete with obstacles, with demonic powers; and that living the Christian faith means a constant struggle against those demonic forces that claim to destroy in the name of the Christian God. Here began Koyama's lifelong struggle with the beast of idolatry, which he refers to as "the boosting of the finite into the infinite." Too often disciples of the various faiths—Christianity is no exception here—invoke the name of God to enhance their own agenda. But when the suffering of God culminating in Christ's death on the cross is fully embraced as the underpinning of one's theology, it should be understood as a divine judgment against all forms of the finite which claim to speak on behalf of the infinite.

Koyama's book *Mount Fuji and Mount Sinai: A Critique of Idols* is, as the title suggests, a study of the many facets of idolatry. Here he uses examples from both Japanese and Christian spirituality. He writes: "If the world of nature-oriented religions produces 'instant gods' then the world that speaks of the 'maker of heaven and earth' often takes the name of God in vain" (p. 240). Both the idols of Mount Fuji and Mount Sinai are capable of destroying the human race. Koyama finds in a "theology of the cross" a prophetic judgment on both the theologies of Mount Fuji and Mount Sinai in their boost of the finite into the infinite. A theology of the cross is a constant reminder of our finitude. It makes us painfully aware of the many finite gods competing for our allegiance, including the gods of national and material superiority, of racism and military might. In his book *No Handle on the Cross*, Koyama continues his critique of idolatry, affirming that any theology that attempts to "put a handle to the power of God is no longer a theology, but a demonic theological ideology" (p. 3). This theme of idolatry remains a key component of Koyama's theology as it does for many Third World liberation theologians.

The second important personal experience that affected Koyama's theological pilgrimage in a profound way was his tenure as a Japanese Kyoda (United Church of Christ in Japan) missionary in Thailand from 1960 to 1968. He refers to this period of his life as his rediscovery of Asia. He came into intimate contact with Thai Theravada Buddhism. During these years he began to live, both literally and figuratively, in East and West, consciously trying to promote creative dialogue and understanding among the cultures and religions of these two radically different areas of the world. In his best-known book, *Waterbuffalo Theology*, Koyama describes how he was forced to find completely new ways of expressing the Christian faith in order to make contact with the Thai people in their everyday lives. Consequently, he developed a whole new terminology designed for Thai consumption, combining imagery from both Theravada Buddhism and Christianity, the result of which was "Thai theology from below." To be sure, he did not invent this theology; it was already there waiting to be born.

Waterbuffalo Theology has made a major contribution toward helping Westerners see that it is absolutely imperative to indigenize theology. Koyama's own experience as a missionary in Thailand gave him a new vision of the different forms that Asian Christianity must take, a vision that has made him increasingly critical of Western missionaries traveling from West to East to instruct Asians in the Christian faith. We must free ourselves, he argues, from both the "Christian superiority complex" and the companion "teachers' complex." By ridding ourselves of these idolatrous Western impediments we can, Koyama believes, begin to open up the possibility of truly genuine and creative encounters with peoples of differing faiths and ideologies.

One final important element of Koyama's theological perspective, to which we have already alluded, is his embrace of the concept of the suffering God. God suffers because God is love. Critical to this conviction of a suffering, caring God is God's vulnerability and openness. "Where there is agape," Koyama affirms, "there is vulnerability." God's vulnerability can best be seen in the suffering of Christ who paradoxically affirms his centrality by "emptying himself" and going to the periphery, to the marginalized and powerless. Christ's strength is made manifest in his weakness, in his giving himself to and for the sake of the poor. The cross of Christ reveals the depths of the suffering, loving God whose "peripheralized power" emerges in the weak and lowly.

Koyama has a deep appreciation for Marxism, although references to Marx in his writings are few and far between. Koyama finds in liberation theology the fundamental conviction of Christian theology that the periphery—the world of the oppressed and vulnerable—is not forsaken by God, but rather is the primary locus of God's loving and suffering presence. Liberation theology is "periphery theology," testifying that "God's weakness is stronger than humanity, and God's foolishness is wiser than humanity."

BOOKS

Waterbuffalo Theology. Maryknoll, N.Y.: Orbis Books, 1974.

No Handle on the Cross. Maryknoll, N.Y.: Orbis Books, 1977.

Three Mile an Hour God. Maryknoll, N.Y.: Orbis Books, 1980.

Mount Fuji and Mount Sinai. Maryknoll, N.Y.: Orbis Books, 1985.

GEEVARGHESE MAR OSTHATHIOS

The task of theology is to reinterpret the contents of the revealed and permanent dogma to the particular needs of each age. There is no dogma more permanent for a Christian understanding of God than the dogma of Holy Trinity. God wants us to look into this venerable dogma again, not as an article of belief, but as one of praxis. Hence God is himself guiding the thinking of theologians as well as of other people to evolve a theology of a classless society (Theology of a Classless Society, *p. 17*).

Geevarghese Mar Osthathios, of the Orthodox church of South India, believes that the doctrine of the Trinity provides the key to a theology of liberation that will unlock the distinctions between individuality and society, authority and freedom, and at the same time provide the necessary framework for a universal society in which individuals can be both distinct and equal.

Mar Osthathios was born in Kerala, India, in 1918. At an early age he experienced a religious conversion and for a time served as a child evangelist with a revival group that traveled through central Travancore in India. Because of his family's poor economic status, Mar Osthathios's education was inferior and sporadic, often interrupted because of the family's economic condition. Fortunately a local religious leader of another denomination recognized his potential and recommended that he enter Leonard Theological College in Jubulpore. He graduated from there in 1947. He then matriculated to Drew University in New Jersey where he received his M.A. degree in religion in 1950. While at Drew, he came under the influence of Stanley Hopper, Carl Michalson, and especially Edwin Lewis whose research on the doctrine of the Trinity in the writings of St. Augustine had a profound impact on Mar Osthathios's evolving theology. He continued his graduate education at Columbia University and Union Theological Seminary and from there he earned an S.T.M. degree in 1951. At Union his mentors included Paul Tillich, Reinhold Niebuhr, and George Florovsky.

Mar Osthathios began teaching at the Orthodox Theological Seminary in Kottayam, Kerala, in 1952, and he continues to lecture there in the areas of Christian ethics, missiology, and modern trends in theology. He was consecrated a bishop in 1975 and serves as Metropolitan of the Orthodox Syrian church in the Niranam diocese. His other major responsibilities have included membership on the Faith and Order Commission of the World Council of Churches, 1974-82; delegate to the World Council of Churches Youth Assembly at Kottayam, 1952; advisor to the World Council of Churches Assembly in Nairobi in 1975; and continuing participation in the Orthodox-Roman Catholic and Orthodox-Lutheran dialogues in India. Since 1972 his close friendship with the German theologian Jürgen Moltmann has been an important contributing factor to his theological development.

Two features dominate his theological convictions. The first is his deep concern to make his Orthodox church a missionary-minded church with a particular concern for the suffering. As early as the 1950s, he deposited all his savings in what has since become St. Paul's Mission Training Center in Kottayam for the purpose of training evangelists. Out of this program have come the founding of orphanages, marriage assistance funds and other projects specifically designed for the poor and needy. In 1987, for example, St. Gregorios Children's Village was established to serve the children of lepers.

This passion for missions focused on service to the needy has led to Mar Osthathios's conviction that human society should eliminate all class distinctions. He even titled one of his books *The Sin of Being Rich in a Poor World.* Here he challenges the wealthy and middle classes to "feel it their bounden duty to see that there are no poor people in the vicinity of the parish and that they are committing a sin when they do not share their wealth with the needy brothers" (p. 3). Mar Osthathios insists that both the rich and the poor desperately need liberation, the former from their callous selfishness and inhumanity, the latter from their exploitation. The ideal would be to meld the rich and poor into a classless society, a goal which Mar Osthathios believes cannot be reached under a capitalistic system. Capitalism, based primarily on the profit motive, is inherently a selfish system that "should be discarded as slavery was discarded long ago and a better structure of social justice must be evolved as early as possible" (p. 5).

But Mar Osthathios does not believe that the solution is to replace capitalism with communism or some other Marxist social order. He is as critical of Marxism as he is of capitalism. Marxism errs in being both atheistic and materialistic. Although he says that the influence of Marxism on his thinking has been meagre and indirect, Mar Osthathios does believe that the Marxist analysis of capitalism as inherently exploitative is correct. He further claims that the U.S. war industry is a leading cause of capitalist exploitation of the poor nations of the Third World. He even suggests that God may have chosen Karl Marx to assist in building a classless society in the same way that God chose Cyrus of Persia to fulfill the divine plan for Israel. Mar Osthathios is convinced that Marxism and capitalism in their present forms, as manifested in Russia and the United States, will either destroy each other or eventually compromise and finally merge into a responsible society based on the universal equitable sharing of God's resources. He opts for what he calls a democratic socialism based on an international economic order and a world government.

The second major feature of Mar Osthathios's version of liberation theology is his ringing affirmation of the doctrine of the Trinity. He admits that he is obsessed with the Trinitarian formula. He considers it to be the linch-pin in solving the longstanding tension between the personal emphasis dominant in capitalism and the social emphasis so important to communism. Here he credits Jürgen Moltmann for sharpening his vision of the implications of the Trinity for human society. The thesis of his best-known book, *Theology of a Classless Society*, is that "only the Christian doctrine of Trinity is the theology come of age and that it has a decisive role to play in everyday experience" (p. 25). Mar Osthathios views the Trinity as a model for a society that extols "equality despite distinctions." God can be construed as a nuclear family of "God the Father, the church the mother, Jesus Christ the elder brother and the whole humanity as direct brothers and sisters" (p. 95). The Trinity has no class distinctions; nor should the church. In the Trinity the three Persons are distinct yet equal, a unity of love in a plurality of freedom. As in the Trinity, in the ideal classless human society there would be "neither selfishness nor jealousy in any member of a perfect home as all live for others and all resources are shared for the common benefit and the benefit of each one" (p. 28).

It is important to note that Mar Osthathios does not derive his advocacy of a classless society from Marxism. Rather, his appreciation of the richness and relevance of the Trinity, together with his own intense awareness of pervasive poverty in the caste-structure of Indian society, have been the determining factors. His affinity for liberation theology becomes crystal clear in his strong condemnation of the unequal and unjust social structures in his native country, which keep the poor in complete submission to the wealthy. But he is not content to develop only an Indian version of liberation theology. He sees real merit in minjung theology coming out of Korea and black theology as manifested in South Africa. He is encouraged by the many small Christian base communities sprouting up all over Asia. He believes that the conscientization process fostered by these small communities is much stronger among Asian people in the 1980s—especially the young—than it was ten years earlier. Yet at the same time, Mar Osthathios is more disillusioned by the intransigence of present-day capitalism and Marxism than he was in the 1970s. Sadly he acknowledges that the rich are becoming richer and the poor are growing poorer.

Mar Osthathios believes that his unique contribution to liberation theology lies in his advocacy of the doctrine of the Trinity as the foundation for building an egalitarian, diverse, sharing and free society. In recent years he has encouraged dialogue in his own country with Muslims and Hindus. Here once again he considers the doctrine of the Trinity an asset, even a bridge-builder among the different faiths. He is fond of quoting the Hindu Radhakrishnan's statement: "Roughly we may say that the Self in its transcendental, cosmic and individual aspects answers to the Christian doctrine of Father, Son and Holy Spirit." Mar Osthathios's hope for the future lies in building a one-world community fashioned after the model of the Holy Trinity.

BOOKS

Most of the books and articles written by Geevarghese Mar Osthathios are in his native Malayalam language. His two books in English are:

Theology of a Classless Society. Maryknoll, N.Y.: Orbis Books, 1980.

The Sin of Being Rich in a Poor World. Madras: The Christian Literature Society, 1983.

ARTICLES

"Conviction of Truth and Tolerance of Love," *International Review of Mission*, Vol. 74, No. 6, Oct. 1985, pp. 490-496.

"Divine Sharing: Shape of Mission for the Future," *International Review of Mission*, Vol. 74, No. 301, Jan. 1987, pp. 16-21.

ALOYSIUS PIERIS

...the theological axis of our deliberations should have, as its two poles, the Third Worldness of our continent and its peculiarly Asian character: two points of reference we must never lose sight of. Spelt out in more realistic terms, the common denominator between Asia and the rest of the Third World is its overwhelming poverty; the specific character which defines Asia within the other poor countries is its multifaceted religiosity. These are two inseparable realities which in their interpenetration constitute what might be designated as the Asian context and which is the matrix of any theology that is truly Asian (Toward an Asian Theology of Liberation: Some Religio-Cultural Guidelines, *p. 75*).

Aloysius Pieris believes that the overwhelming poverty suffered by the teeming masses on the Asian continent, combined with religious pluralism which renders the Christian community but a tiny minority, provide the distinctive framework for an Asian theology of liberation. It is this dialectic between poverty and its multi-faith setting that makes Asian forms of liberation theology so different from their Latin American and African counterparts.

Pieris was born in Ampitiya, Ceylon, now Sri Lanka, in 1934. He entered the Society of Jesus at the age of nineteen and was ordained a priest in 1965. His graduate degrees include a L. Ph. degree from Sacred Heart College, Shembaganur, India, in 1959; a B.A. in Sanskrit and Pali from the University of London in 1961, and an S.T.L. degree from the Pontifical Theological Faculty in Naples in 1966. He also studied prepolyphonic music in Venice.

Reared in a country that is predominantly Buddhist, Pieris soon realized that to work effectively as a priest in his homeland, he would have to study Buddhism. In 1972 he became the first Christian to earn a Ph.D. degree in Buddhist philosophy from the University of Sri Lanka. During these university years he also practied meditation under the supervision of a Buddhist monk, a practice which he continues. He then taught Buddhist philosophy for a year at the Gregorian University in Rome, but decided that he must return home and get a thorough acquaintance with Buddhist practices.

Pieris proceeded to set up his own community near the Buddhist University of Kelenia north of Colombo, which later evolved into the Tulana Research Center of which he is director. The purpose of this center is to encourage dialogue between Buddhists and Christians on the threefold basis of the experience of popular religion, philosophical-textual study, and pastoral reflection in the context of social transformation. Although his Jesuit order bought the original property, Pieris has since refused further financial support, preferring that the Center be entirely independent and make its own way from the earnings of its own members. Pieris also serves as professor of Asian Religions at the East Asia Pastoral Institute in Manila.

Pieris credits the Second Vatican Council with giving him the impetus to seek out new areas of cooperation between Buddhism and Christianity. Two other experiences are paramount in providing additional encouragement in this direction. The first was the difficulty he had in being permitted as a Christian to study Buddhism at the Buddhist University of Sri Lanka. In the late 1960s animosity between Christians and Buddhists was high, fueled in large part by the superior attitude of Christian missionaries. Pieris had a difficult time convincing the Buddhist authorities that his intentions for studying Buddhism were honorable "till one day, garbed in my cassock as a Catholic priest, I took a basket of fruit and flowers and, in the presence of a Buddhist leader, I fell prostrate. I worshipped him and asked to be accepted as his pupil. From that day, I have had no problem with Buddhist monks" ("Toward a Liberating Asian Theology and Spirituality," p. 43).

The second experience, far more harsh, occurred about the same time and helped him see the absolute centrality of social justice issues. After years of turmoil, Ceylon's struggle to free itself from British colonial rule culminated in the successful revolution of 1972, when Ceylon declared itself a republic and changed its name to Sri Lanka. During this tumultuous prelude to independence, the government of Ceylon was closely linked with the Buddhist establishment which controlled much of the land and wealth. As a result, large numbers of young people—mostly university students—became disenchanted both with their government and the Buddhist leaders. They turned to Marxism. Pieris himself sought to open the lines of communication with some of these students. One student in particular helped Pieris realize the idolatry of defending his own church which, like the Buddhist establishment, too often favored the rich and showed little concern for the poor. Pieris came to a new understanding of God and God's special concern for the poor. "I am preaching about an unjust god who doesn't exist. In a way, I am preaching atheism —because God is just and nobody is just if he is not favorable to the poor...my Buddhist experience of total poverty detachment, of going deep to experience, of denying everything and accepting and rediscovering God in a new dimension, and then coming back to this reality of the social dimension, of gross injustice...have contributed to my personal synthesis" (pp. 47-48).

As a result of these experiences and his synthesis of the demands of poverty with his Buddhist-Christian dialogue, Pieris has, since the late 1960s, forged his own distinctive version of liberation theology. It has been a challenge to Western forms of the Christian faith as well as to Latin American and African versions. Consider, for example, Pieris's new understanding of the proper relationship between Christianity and Buddhism. Pieris believes that "deep within each of us there is a Buddhist and a Christian engaged in a profound encounter which each tradition—Buddhist and Christian—has registered in the doctrinal articulation of its core-experience" ("Christianity and Buddhism in Core-to-Core Dialogue," p. 51). While Buddhism stresses *gnosis* or liberative knowledge, Christianity emphasizes *agape* or redemptive love. These two dimensions are by no means contradictory. In fact, they are "complementary idioms that need each other to mediate the self-transcending experience called salvation" (p. 48). Salvation, Pieris contends, not the doctrine of God, should be the basis for theology. For the Buddhist, God-talk is nonsensical. But for both Buddhist and Christian, salvation and liberation are central and intimately connected. "The core of any religion is the liberating experience which brought that religion into being. A religion would die as soon as it was born if it failed to evolve some means of perpetuating the accessibility of this experience" (p. 57). Pieris uses the terms *ascent buddhology* and *descent buddhology* to suggest that in using the *ascent* approach that starts with human experience, Buddhists and Christians discover many similarities along the pathway of salvation. Pieris also speaks of the "theology of double baptism" by which he means baptism both in "the Jordan of Asian Religiosity and baptism in the Calvary of Asian Poverty" ("Toward a Liberating Asian Theology and Spirituality," p. 45).

In affirming the importance of creative dialogue between Buddhists and Christians at the grassroots level, Pieris expands the notion of the Christian base communities of Latin America to become *human* base communities in Asia. Membership in these communities should include members of all religious faiths who share the blight of poverty and oppression. "Any liberation theology begins to be formulated only when a given Christian community begins to be drawn into the local peoples' struggle for full humanity and through that struggle begins to sink its roots in the lives and cultures of these people, most of whom, in our continent, happen to be non-Christian" ("A Theology of Liberation in Asian Churches?" p. 117). These basic human communities are emerging in Asia on the periphery of the established churches and are forging their own oriental spirituality. In Sri Lanka several such communities have become prominent, including the Satoyada group under the leadership of the Jesuit Paul Casperz in Kandy; the Devasarana monastery led by the Anglican monk Yohan Devananda; the community at Buttala established by Father Michael Rodrigo; and the Christian Workers' Fellowship, which has branches throughout Sri Lanka. Pieris believes that these human base communities are "expanding the existing boundaries of orthodoxy in the very process of entering into the liberative streams of other religions and cultures" ("The Place of Non-Christian Religions and Cultures in the Evolution of a Third World Theology," p. 5).

Pieris does not hesitate to use Marxist analysis as a tool for understanding the causes of poverty. But liberation involves much more than class struggle. "Marxism needs to be humanized by Christianity. Christianity needs to be radicalized by Marxism." Here the dimension of spirituality—what Pieris often calls the *introspective* component—looms large. Pieris insists: "A liberation theopraxis in Asia which uses only the Marxist tools of social analysis will remain un-Asian and ineffective until it integrates the psychological tools of *introspection* which our sages have discovered." However, Pieris does believe very strongly that there should be a more equitable sharing of the earth's resources. This explains "the liberation theologian's political option for socialism, i.e., for a definite social order in which oppressive structures are changed radically, even violently, in order to allow every person to be fully human, the assumption being that no one is liberated until everyone is" ("Toward an Asian Theology of Liberation: Some Religio-Cultural Guidelines," pp. 88, 90).

For Aloysius Pieris the "irruption of the Third World is also the irruption of the non-Christian world" ("The Place of Non-Christian Religions and Cultures in the Evolution of Third World Theology," p. 113). It is this latter fact that demands a new theological methodology. To that end, Pieris sees as his responsibility to help the churches *in* Asia become churches *of* Asia by linking arms with the adherents of other religions in forging base *human* communities. The primary mission of these communities would be to liberate the poor from their miseries.

BOOK

An Asian Theology of Liberation. Maryknoll, N.Y.: Orbis Books, 1988.

ARTICLES

"Monastic Poverty in the Asian Setting," *Dialogue*, 7, 1980, pp. 104-118.

"Towards an Asian Theology of Liberation: Some Religio-Cultural Guidelines," *Asia's Struggle for Full Humanity*. Edited by Virginia Fabella. Maryknoll, N.Y.: Orbis Books, 1980, pp. 75-96.

"The Asian Sense in Theology," *Living Theology in Asia*. Edited by John C. England. Maryknoll, N.Y.: Orbis Books, 1982, pp. 171-176.

"The Place of Non-Christian Religions and Cultures in the Evolution of a Third World Theology," *East Asian Pastoral Review*, Vol. 19, No. 2, 1982, pp. 5-34. Also, in *The Irruption of the Third World: Challenge to Theology*. Maryknoll, N.Y.: Orbis Books, 1983, pp. 113-140.

"The Political Vision of the Buddhists," *Dialogue*, 11, 1984, pp. 6-14.

"Western Models of Inculturation: How Far Are They Applicable in Non-Semitic Asia?" *East Asian Pastoral Review*, Vol. 22, No. 2, 1985, pp. 116-125.

"Toward a Liberating Asian Theology and Spirituality," *Ang Makato*, Vol. 3, December-January 1986, pp. 43-51.

"A Theology of Liberation in Asian Churches?" *East Asian Pastoral Review*, Vol. 23, No. 2, 1986, pp. 117-138.

"Christianity and Buddhism in Core-to-Core Dialogue," *Cross Currents*, Vol. 37, No. 1, 1987, pp. 47-76.

"The Buddha and the Christ: Mediators of Liberation," *The Myth of Christian Uniqueness: Toward a Pluralistic Theology of Religions*. Edited by John Hick and Paul F. Knitter. Maryknoll, N.Y.: Orbis Books, 1987, pp. 162-177.

Samuel Rayan

Christian theologians in India have to fulfill a function vis-a-vis the Christian community as well as the entire national community. Our own search for a theology must take into account all other searches and movements for liberation. This we do in conversation with historically relevant reinterpretations and fresh insights of Hindu, Muslim, Buddhist and Christian theologies while safeguarding the uniqueness of each. New liberative interpretations of religious tenets and symbols are beginning to appear in all the great spiritual traditions of our country, bearing the promise of a living theology at the service of the people (Theological Priorities in India Today, *pp. 31, 35*).

Samuel Rayan presents a major theme of Asian liberation theology, namely, the importance of placing the Christian religion in the context of the other major living religions of the East. As a liberation theologian Samuel Rayan is committed to helping Christians throughout India discover the communitarian/egalitarian dimensions of the aspirations of people of all religions, especially those who suffer from poverty and oppression. In so doing Rayan also hopes that his work can help the people of the United States reflect critically on their own country's abuse of power: what the United States has done and continues to do to oppress the blacks, the Native Americans,the poor of Central America, as well as other impoverished people throughout the Third World.

Samuel Rayan's concern for the poor and oppressed and his deep appreciation for the spiritual heritage of Hinduism and Buddhism in his native country are very much a product of his own life history. He was born in Kumbalam, Kerala State, India, in 1920. Two events deeply influenced his early years: India's struggle for national liberation from British colonial domination and the successful though painful victory of the depressed Ezhava community of the State of Kerala in finally winning their social and economic liberation from age-old discrimination and humiliation that had been based on caste prejudice. Thus Samuel Rayan from his early years knew firsthand of the cruelties of oppression and unjust treatment of the poor and the marginalized who kept fighting for survival and human dignity. In the midst of all this pain he also came to know the power of an intense spirituality exhibited in the lives of such men as Sri Narayana Guru and Mohandas Gandhi, individuals who were able to retain their serenity in the midst of suffering. So the attitudes and perceptions about life that Rayan experienced during these years lie at the basis of his own theological views which were only to emerge later.

Rayan grew up in a distinctly Catholic atmosphere within a culture that was pervaded by Hinduism. In this context he developed an absorbing interest in all the facets of religion, including liturgy, prayer, the Bible, the saints, and even Hindu myths and stories. This religious sensibility, together with his awareness of the poverty and oppression that surrounded him in the caste-ridden Hindu society, instilled in him the dream of a society based on human equality and dignity, a dream that has remained with him throughout his life. It was later in his life with the benefit of hindsight that he realized how these attitudes and dreams tallied with his understanding of the Christian faith and how a theology of liberation lay latent in the ongoing struggles of the oppressed.

Samuel Rayan entered the Society of Jesus in 1939 and was ordained a priest in 1955. He has earned degrees in philosophy from Sacred Heart College, Madurai (1946), in literature from the Kerala University (1950) in India, and a doctorate in theology from the Gregorian University in Rome (1960). He has served as Chaplain to the All India Catholic University Federation, Kerala Sector, from 1960 to 1972; and professor of systematic theology at the faculty of theology, Vidyajyoti Institute of Religious Studies, Delhi, from 1972 to the present. He has been a member of the Commission on Faith and Order of the World Council of Churches and is one of the editors of *Jeevadhara*, a journal of Christian Interpretation.

Two factors are of particular importance in understanding Samuel Rayan's theological development. The first is that during his 12 years as chaplain to the more than fifteen thousand Catholic university students at the university in Karala, his political and social interests became pronounced and consciously linked with his theological views. He realized that faith, to be meaningful, had social-political repercussions. As he suggested: "Living and searching with fiercely honest youth helped make theology earthly-historical and render the Bible open-ended, unfinished." The second factor was his growing interest in literature—especially poetry and myth—which developed in him a feel for religious symbolism as well as a sense of mystery pervading all things. This factor—which he himself traces back to his rural peasant culture—helped him rise above any narrow view of religious orthodoxy and enabled him to discern the spiritual potential in Asian religious traditions.

Rayan is engaged in forging what he calls an inductive-liberationist method in theology, beginning "from below." By articulating a theological basis for collaborating among followers of all faiths and ideologies, a common effort can be made for the liberation of the downtrodden and the building of a free and equal social order for all people. Theology today must give priority to praxis and experience over theory and external authority. In recent years, Rayan has given increasing attention to what he calls "atheism that comes clothed in religious garb," that is, idolatrous forms of religion that give allegiance to finite principalities and powers, and to commodity culture and mammon.

Rayan is especially critical of the idolatrous gods of capitalism and colonialism, the former with its continuing history of violence in favoring profits over people, the latter of which has kept the powerless poor in subjection. He has found in Marxist social analysis a useful tool for evaluating the weaknesses of capitalism and colonialism and the power that the economic system has as a means of enslaving or liberating human beings. Rayan is also aware of the limitations of Marxism in applying Marx's Western categories to the Asian setting. Yet he still ponders: "I am beginning to see that liberation theology in Asia or anywhere cannot ignore the fact that it is people inspired by Marxism that have successfully resisted imperialism's armed might in Asia and in most other parts of the world. Does this fact have no theological significance, I am beginning to ask myself."

Samuel Rayan believes that all religions carry a latent theology of liberation. So do all the struggles for freedom and dignity, whether they be the struggles of ancient slaves, colonized peoples, oppressed classes or despised cultures. The marginalized peoples of the Third World hold their faith and their life together. Rayan senses an increased awakening and reaching out for freedom on the part of these people, a movement that will continue to grow. It is the task of the liberation theologians to support the people in their aspirations and to articulate the theological content of their dreams.

BOOKS AND PAMPHLETS

The Holy Spirit: Heart of the Gospel and Christian Hope. Maryknoll, N.Y.: Orbis Books, 1978.

Anger of God. Bombay: Build, 1982.

In Christ: The Power of Women. Madras: All Indian Council of Christian Women, 1986.

ARTICLES

"The Justice of God," *Living Theology in Asia.* Edited by John C. England. Maryknoll, N.Y.: Orbis Books, 1981, pp. 211-220.

"Theological Priorities in India Today," *Irruption of the Third World.* Edited by Virginia Fabella and Sergio Torres. Maryknoll, N.Y.: Orbis Books, 1983, pp. 30-42.

"Naming the Unnameable," *Naming God.* Edited by R.P. Scharlemann. New York: Paragon Press, 1985, pp. 3-28.

"Baptism and Conversion: The Lima Text in the Indian Context," *A Call to Discipleship*. Edited by G.R. Singh. Delhi: I.S.P.C.K., 1985, pp. 166-187.

"Jesus and Imperialism," *Jesus Today*. Edited by S. Kappen. Madras: AI-CUF House, 1985. (Rayan has five other articles in this book.)

"Interculturation and the Local Church," *Mission Studies* 3, No. 2, 1986.

"Irruption of the Poor: Challenge to Theology," *Concilium* 187, No. 5, 1986.

CHOAN-SENG SONG

There is another kind of theology, of the Chuang Tzu type. It's a theology capable of transportation. Just as Chuang Tzu puts himself in the position of the fish and perceives its state of being, this kind of theology crosses the boundaries of cultures, religions, and histories in order to have deeper contacts with the strange and mysterious ways and thoughts of God in creation. In the case of Chuang Tzu, his picture of the universe is not complete until he takes into his confidence other creatures that share with him this vast creation. Should not theology also be ready to transpose itself into unfamiliar situations to be confronted by the bewildering but gracious ways of God with all creation? (The Compassionate God, p. xii).

Crossing the boundaries of cultures, religions and histories has been one of the major contributions of Choan-Seng Song to liberation theology. In so doing, Song seeks to liberate theology from its western captivity by utilizing the resources of Asia. He speaks of a "Third-Eye theology," a power of perception and intuition that focuses on compassion at the heart of religion, and cuts across the boundaries of culture, religion, and history.

Choan-Seng Song was born in Taiwan in 1929. He earned his undergraduate degree in philosophy from National Taiwan University and his ministerial degree from New College, University of Edinburgh in Scotland. He received his Ph.D. degree from Union Theological Seminary in New York City in 1965. He has taught Old Testament and systematic theology at Tainan Theological College where he also served as Principal from 1965 to 1970. He served as Associate Director of the Faith and Order Commission of the World Council of Churches from 1973 to 1982, and was Director of Studies, World Alliance of Reformed Churches, from 1983 to 1986. He serves as professor of theology and Asian cultures at Pacific School of Religion and he is also professor of theology and Dean of the program for theology and culture at the South East Asia Graduate School of Theology.

Song cites two major events in his earlier years as having a profound impact on his theological development. The first was his return to Taiwan and his exposure to the religions and cultures of Taiwan and its Chinese heritage *after* his theological training in the West. This experience opened his eyes to the realization that Christian theology had been prisoner to "the Latin captivity of the church." These years in Taiwan convinced him that theology had to be couched in Asian symbols and stories if it is to make sense to the daily lives of the Asian people. Thus, indigenization—the central theme in his book, *Theology from the Womb of Asia* — became central to his theological mission.

The second catalyst in Song's theological development was his personal involvement in the political struggles over the future of Taiwan and its relationship to the Chinese mainland. Song was especially sensitive to the fact that it was the poor who suffered the most in these struggles. He was one of the four initiators of a movement called "Formosan Christians for Self-determination." This involvement in the political destiny of the poor people of his native country helped him to understand the Bible and the role of Jesus Christ "from the bottom up," as he puts it, an experience that has been common among Third World liberation theologians. And it also made him much more aware of the spirit of the liberator God present in a society that had never been a part of the Christian tradition. Surely, Song maintains, "God must be capable of hearing, understanding, and responding to the cries of humanity uttered in different languages, the hopes and despairs expressed in diverse cultures and religious symbols. Christian theology has barely begun to hear and understand these languages and symbols" (*The Compassionate God*, p. 167).

According to Song, the primary task of Asian liberation theology is to help Christian churches expand their vision of how God is at work in the Asian setting where Christians are but a small minority. To that end Asian symbols taken from non-Christian religions become an important vehicle for communication. For example, the symbol of the Buddha or Bodhisattva sitting cross-legged on the lotus is as important to a proper appreciation of Asian spirituality as the cross is to Christians. The Christian churches have a responsibility to infuse the love of God found in Jesus Christ with the spirituality found in Asian religions.

To accomplish this task, Song argues that Asian theology must be done by Asian theologians who have had their roots in the lives of the Asian poor and oppressed. For this reason Latin American liberation theology cannot be imported, any more than can classical Western theology. Here Song sides with those theologians who uphold the significance of cultural liberation as equally important, if not more so, than socio-political issues. Song makes great use of Asian stories and symbols, for example, the lotus, the tears of Lady Meng, the dream of Emperor Ming, the chains of karma, hibiki, Bodhisattva, and so on.

Marxism cannot succeed as an import from the western world any more than can western versions of religion. To be sure, Marx's critique of religion has been important to Song in his assessment of religion and its relationship to social and economic forces. But Marxism as an ideology transplanted to Asia operates as a foreign intruder impervious to the Asian cultural setting. Moreover, the Mao Zedong version of Marxism in China with its radical political and social vision makes Song even more critical of Marxism as a viable option for Asian societies.

One of Song's major concerns has been to expand the meaning of liberation, the liberation of the Third-Eye, which inspires a theology of the head to include a religion of the heart. Such emancipation encompasses freedom from ourselves and our own partial histories as well as freedom from institutional rigidities. And by all means Asia—and Song would also point the finger here at the United States with its religious pluralism—must be liberated from traditional Christian provincialism. Maybe, Song says, we have reached the point where we should stop criticizing other religions and turn our attack against our own creeds and hymns which are so utterly boring. Christian missions do not need to be "Christianizing" missions. We don't have to go around baptizing everyone. Song asks: "Is there not much counterfeit theology going around in Asia? Our theology becomes counterfeit when it says Hinduism does not know the true God because it is lost in a pantheon of many gods and many Lords. Buddhism has no God because it teaches salvation by one's own power" (*Theology from the Womb of Asia*, p. 59). Christian theology, Song believes, is still in its infancy when it comes to appreciating the symbols and the truth-value to be found in other religions. Here again, cultural liberation is the key.

For Song, real flesh-and-blood theology does not begin with theological pronouncements from on high. It begins with people in their everyday lives. "Humanity to theology is something like water to fish. Fish die when taken out of water. Theology dies when divorced from human life and history." God is the Power of Hope for those who suffer, the Power of Hope for "the poor and the rich, the oppressed and the oppressors, the theists and the atheists, Christians, Muslims, Jews, Buddhists, and Hindus" (*The Compassionate God*, p. 260). It is this kind of faith and hope that enables all of us "to see the vision of tomorrow in the darkness of today" (*Theology from the Womb of Asia*, p. 216).

BOOKS

Prelude to a New Era. Taiwan: The Presbyterian Church Press, 1962.

A Christian Understanding of Man. Taiwan: Tunghai University Press, 1965.

The Church: Its Task and Future. Taiwan: The Presbyterian Church Press, 1970.

Third-Eye Theology: Theology in Formation in Asian Settings. Maryknoll, N. Y.: Orbis Books, 1979.

The Tears of Lady Meng: A Parable of People's Political Theology. Maryknoll, N. Y.: Orbis Books, 1982.

The Compassionate God. Maryknoll, N.Y.: Orbis Books, 1982.

Tell Us Our Names. Maryknoll, N. Y.: Orbis Books, 1984.

Theology from the Womb of Asia. Maryknoll, N.Y.: Orbis Books, 1986.

ARTICLES

"From Israel to Asia: A Theological Leap," *Ecumenical Review*, Vol. 28, No. 3, July 1976, pp. 252-265.

"A Journey of Faith: The Ecumenical Task of Reformed Theology," *Reformed World*, Vol. 38, No. 2, June 1984, pp. 105-118.

"The Power of God's Grace in the World of Religions," *The Ecumenical Review*, Vol. 39, No. 1, January 1987, pp. 44-65.

PART III

LATIN AMERICA

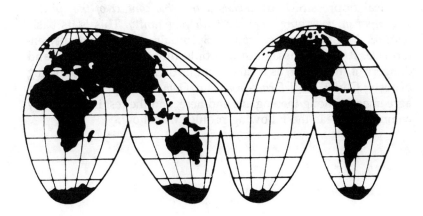

North American readers are more acquainted with the Latin American version of Third World liberation theology than with the African and Asian types. This is to be expected inasmuch as Latin America is "closer to home" and more has been written in English about its theological developments. In recognition of this fact, I have included here profiles of 16 Latin American liberation theologians.

When one mentions Latin American theology, one immediately thinks of Gustavo Gutiérrez, rightly judged to be the premier Third World liberation theologian. His *A Theology of Liberation* (1973) has been for most of us the launching pad for our introduction to liberation theology. But Gustavo Gutiérrez would be the first to admit that he is neither the architect of liberation theology nor its only major spokesperson. This is why Michael Novak's comment about liberation theology is absurd: "Only a few theologians—in this case, led by Gustavo Gutiérrez and Juan Luis Segundo—do the lion's share of the innovation: most of the rest is commentary" (*Freedom with Justice: Catholic Social Thought and Liberation Institutions.* San Francisco: Harper & Row, 1984, p. 183). Of course, Gutiérrez and Segundo have done pioneering work, but Novak's naiveté about liberation theology causes him to overlook the distinctive contributions of many other important Latin American liberation theologians who are included here.

Latin American liberation theology zeroes in on socio-economic-political oppression, but *always within the context of the spiritual component emerging from the faith community*. This is its basic feature. As Gutiérrez maintains: "Spirituality is a community enterprise. It is the passage of a people through the solitude and dangers of the desert, as it carves out its own way in the following of Jesus Christ" (*We Drink from Our Own Wells*, p. 137). But the agreements among theologians end here, and the rest is not merely commentary—as the following profiles will show.

Hugo Assmann

Commitment to the process of liberation in Latin America means starting from a particular analysis of our situation as oppressed peoples; that opting for a particular social analysis is not a neutral step. It involves the necessary choice of an ethical and political stance; there is no such thing as an uninvolved social science, and to pretend that there is is itself to adopt a reactionary ideological position. This fact has already become central to discussions of methodology on the level of the social sciences. There is probably no more obvious example of a committed science anywhere today than sociology in Latin America, which has taken the decisive step of making "dependence" the central theme of its investigations into the real situation in Latin America. This situation of dependence is the basic starting-point for the process of liberation (Theology for a Nomad Church, *pp. 129-130*).

Hugo Assmann has made his major contribution to liberation theology in his capacity as a sociologist-theologian who, like Otto Maduro, insists that theology is never devoid of a specific historical and temporal setting. Anyone who thinks that theology can escape social conditioning has unwittingly become the prisoner of a particular ideology. This claim has been directed in particular to theologians of the First World who often declare that their theology is pure and untainted when, in fact, it is usually colored by affluence and a capitalist ideology.

Hugo Assmann was born in Venâncio Aires, Rio Grande de Sul, Brazil, in 1933. From an early age, his exposure to poverty and oppression seared his conscience and provided the foundation for his later identification with the struggles of the lower classes. After studying philosophy and sociology in his native country, he continued his graduate work in Europe. After writing his thesis on "The Social Dimension of Sin," he received his doctorate in theology from the Gregorian University in Rome. He also earned a licentiate in sociology from the University of Frankfurt and a diploma in communications from the University of Santiago, Chile. He taught theology at the Catholic University of Porto Alegre and in the Jesuit theologate of São Leopoldo, both in Brazil, from 1962 to 1965. From 1967 to 1970, he served as visiting professor at the University of Münster. He then returned to Latin America where for a year he was a member of a research group in Oruro, Bolivia, investigating the oppressive conditions of the Bolivian miners.

During the 1970s, Assmann became radicalized in his political and theological views as he identified more and more with the masses of people at the bottom of the social ladder. His activities on behalf of the poor finally led to his banishment from his native Brazil—and later from Chile, Bolivia, and Uruguay. In 1974 he became professor in the school of journalism at the University of Costa Rica in San José, as well as professor in the National University's department of religious studies. He also was on the staff of the university's research institute, which concentrated on the analysis of social problems, and he was the founder of the Department Ecumenics de Investigaciones (DEI).

Assmann maintains that the founding of DEI was "the best thing I have done in my life as a theologian," and he describes DEI as "the launching pad for innovative, in-depth studies in various theological themes." Assmann considers the DEI's contributions in the areas of "theology and economics, the God of life and the idolatry of the system, the spiritual power of the poor, the importance of specific areas of oppression (of women, blacks, Indians) and ecotheology" especially important.

After twelve years of exile, Assmann was permitted to return to Brazil in 1981 where he now teaches in the areas of the philosophy of education and the social scienses at the Methodist University of Piracicaba. He is also in charge of the campus ministry in his diocese and frequently acts as consultant to base Christian communities. These communities, together with his active involvement in the Worker Party, provide the nourishment for his "new way of doing theology."

Hugo Assmann's basic interest is in utilizing the tools of social analysis to help the people of the lower social classes develop their own "people's version of theology." Such a theology, emerging from the grassroots, must inevitably be contextual and based on praxis, not theory. This means that theology must of necessity be partial and pluralistic, for no theology can have a pure and unadulterated "God's eye" view. Even Latin America itself can have no one theological stance. Assmann has become increasingly impatient with theoreticians of liberation theology who are constantly trying to pigeon-hole Latin American liberation theology into one over-arching theological system, thereby falling victim to the same trap as classical Western theology. The real danger here is that liberation will come to be understood as a movement of ideas. Assmann contends: "It is a great mistake to attempt to understand what liberation theology is and represents by way of a consideration of authors and their writings. If the theology of liberation has acquired a genuine importance for the poor and believing people of our Latin America, this is principally owing to the fact that liberation theology, before all else, is an enormous movement of renewal of the concrete practice of faith, an organized concatenation of options from a departure in the faith experience of the poor, and in a deeper sense, an authentic movement of spirituality. Any attempt to analyse the theology of liberation as a movement of ideas is indicative of a failure to understand its principal dimension, which is spiritual and pastoral."

Assmann has also underscored the need for an adequate christology for Latin America, a view which he shares with Leonardo Boff and others. It is inevitable that there be a conflict of christologies in the church because of different historical and social conditions. Assmann places these christologies within two camps:

the Christ of the reactionaries, the defenders of the "authorized Christ" who support the status quo; and the Christ of the revolutionaries whose aim is to liberate the oppressed from the status quo. Conflict between the two camps is to be expected. "Let us face this fact: faith in a Christ the Liberator, whose liberating power is vitally involved in class struggles and 'takes sides' with the oppressed, inevitably collides with all the Christs of the oppressor classes. And these have them in abundance, for they fabricate them according to the needs of the moment (" The Actuation of the Power of Christ in History," pp. 127-128). The revolutionary Christ, the Liberator, does not hesitate to identify himself with the poor in their struggles for liberation.

Like Gustavo Gutiérrez, Hugo Assmann sees three meanings to the term liberation: political liberation, historical liberation as a result of human beings taking charge of their own destiny, and the liberation from sin that is found in Christ. And what is paramount here, as it is for Third World liberation theologians in general, is the spiritual component *from which all other dimensions of liberation are derived*. Assmann explains that "Liberation theology obviously does not pretend to be an economic theory, although it implies a series of economic reevaluations. It is essentially a strong movement of spirituality growing out of faith experiences in the grassroots" (" Democracy and the Debt Crisis," p. 84).

As a social scientist, Assmann obviously makes use of Marxist social analysis in critiquing the profit motive and the developmentalist theory. The fact of dependence is "the basic starting point for the process of liberation." But Assmann is less pro-Marxist than he is anti-capitalist. "The question is neither capitalism nor socialism. First of all, in about all Latin American countries, no socialism exists presently or around the corner. What does exist is an absolutely savage and inhuman form of 'capitalism'" ("Democracy and the Debt Crisis," p. 92). Assmann is devastating in his criticism of the results of the capitalist system in Latin America. "In terms of destroyed lives, each year we have a devastation equal to that of the Second World War, which totaled five years" (p. 95).

If there is one feature of Assmann's theology of liberation that should be singled out—one so central to theologians of liberation— it is the theme of idolatry. Idolatry is rampant in the gods of the oppressors with their power to exploit and dominate and kill. For this reason the gods of the rich and the God of the poor can never be the same God. Assmann maintains: "The job of being God is not all that pleasant, because there is no way to escape the games of the counterfeiters and their hollowed idols...the oppressed of all the centuries, when they set out to struggle, always discovered many things about the identity of the counterfeiters, and the reasons for the counterfeiting. No one can any longer deceive the poor of our America about this: the god of the rich and the God of the poor are not the same divinity!" (" The Faith of the Poor in Their Struggle with Idols," p. 204).

BOOKS

Theology for a Nomad Church. Maryknoll, N.Y.: Orbis Books, 1976.

A Igreja Electrônica e sen Impacto na America Latina, 1986.

ARTICLES

"Statement by Hugo Assmann," *Theology in the Americas*. Edited by Sergio Torres and John Eagleson. Maryknoll, N.Y.: Orbis Books, 1976, pp. 209-304.

"The Power of Christ in History: Conflicting Christologies and Discernment," *Frontiers of Theology in Latin America*. Edited by Rosino Gibellini. Maryknoll, N.Y.: Orbis Books, 1979, pp. 133-151.

"The Faith of the Poor in Their Struggle with Idols," *The Idols of Death and the God of Life*. Edited by Pablo Richard et. al. Maryknoll, N.Y.: Orbis Books, 1983, pp. 194-231.

"The Actuation of the Power of Christ in History: Notes on the Discernment of Christological Contradiction," *Faces of Jesus*. Edited by José Míguez Bonino. Maryknoll, N.Y.: Orbis Books, 1984, pp. 125-137.

"Democracy and the Debt Crisis," *This World*, Spring-Summer 1986, No. 14, pp. 83-104.

CLODOVIS BOFF

The theology of liberation finds its point of departure, its milieu and its finality in praxis. Its intent is to develop an engaged liberation theology, to which it ascribes a political option, and which it subordinates to praxis. The latter, in the eyes of the theology of liberation, holds the primacy over all theory, indeed is the criterion of the verification of theology. Liberation theology considers praxis as the fundamental locus of theology, the "place" where theology occurs. Finally, liberation theology maintains the reality of a permanent dialectic between theory and practice here: a dialectic between theological theory, and the political praxis of faith (Theology and Praxis, pp. xxi-xxii).

Clodovis Boff's special contribution to liberation theology has to do with methodology, the subject of his doctoral thesis. His intention is to provide an epistemological and ontological framework for a theology of liberation, to show how it differs from the assumptions of classical Western theology.

Clodovis Boff was born in Concórdia, Santa Catarina, Brazil, in 1944. Like his brother, Leonardo, he had direct exposure to poverty and, thanks to his school teacher father, a heightened awareness of the injustices all around him. He studied philosophy in Rio de Janeiro and was ordained a Servite priest. Clodovis Boff then traveled to Europe to study theology at the University of Louvain. Before completing his doctorate, however, he returned to his native country, where from 1969 to 1973—a period he considers the darkest years of the Brazilian dictatorship—he lived in the outlying slums of São Paulo and there began to radically question his own role as a Catholic priest. He studied philosophy at the University of São Paulo, receiving his licentiate in philosophy in 1970. This period was crucial in the development of Boff's theology. In Boff's own words: "The light only dawned when, in a course on the situation in Brazil, the scales fell from my eyes and I realized—through a 'dialectical reading' of society—that the prevailing system was producing a *perverse* development; at the same time as it was producing a great deal of wealth in a small number of people, it was creating more and more and more misery for the great majority of the people."

When Boff returned to the University of Louvain to complete his doctorate, which he received in 1976, he "felt the need to launch a theoretical attack on the problems that such a situation posed to the human conscience, to faith, and to the understanding of faith." The immediate result was his doctoral dissertation, *Theology and Praxis: Epistemological Foundations*.

Boff returned to Brazil where he became, in turn, professor of theology at the Franciscan Theological Institute in Petrópolis; master of the young religious of the Order of the Servites of Mary at São Paulo; and professor of theology at the Pontifical Catholic University of Rio de Janeiro. In 1978, he assumed his present position as professor of theology at Our Lady of the Assumption Faculty of Theology at the Catholic University of São Paulo. He also serves as theological advisor to the Brazilian Conference of Religious.

Clodovis Boff reflects the lifestyle of many Latin American liberation theologians. In recent years he has attached less prestige to his role as a university professor and more importance to his responsibilities as a pastor working with the poor in Christian base communities. His book, *Feet-on-the-Ground Theology: A Brazilian Journey* (1987), suggests a theology that is "worked out with the feet, moves through the whole body, and rises to the head. There are some things you can grasp only by going there and seeing for yourself. This theology says what it has seen and heard as it moved about in the midst of the people" (p. xi). This kind of theology emerges from the grassroots, from "those who live on the rock bottom of history, the poor and the oppressed" (p. xii). Boff goes on to say: "In these poor forest dwellers the kingdom of God is manifest with more power and truth than in the most mystical pontifical liturgies" (p. 48).

It is obvious that this "feet-on-the-ground theology" focuses on the social, economic, and political dimensions of faith, for it is at this horizontal level that the poor experience their greatest oppression. But by no means does this horizontal dimension eliminate the vertical component. Boff is emphatic on this point. "By all means, the transcendent dimension of faith (liberation from sin and communion with the Father by grace), so well developed by classical theology, is enthusiastically and unhesitatingly accepted by the theology of liberation. Indeed, it is in virtue of this transcendent dimension that a liberation *theology* is possible at all" (*Liberation Theology: From Dialogue to Confrontation*, p. 17). Boff believes it is absolutely crucial that the horizontal and vertical dimensions be kept together. "Specifically, to me as a theologian the great task seems to be to *investigate in depth* the relationship between the Kingdom and society, i.e., salvation and liberation."

Marxism plays only a secondary role in Clodovis Boff's theology. It can be a useful tool as an instrument of social analysis. Boff admits that he and other liberation theologians have not always been vocal enough in pointing out the defects of Marxism, especially its materialistic and atheistic components. Marxism's most glaring weakness is that it is concerned only for the horizontal dimension. For precisely this reason, Christian social analysis is much more thoroughgoing in its insistence on the transcendental and spiritual components. Boff underscores this point. "By no means is Marxism the moving force, basis, or inspiration of the theology of liberation. Christian faith is. It is the Gospel that is the determining qualifier of the theology of liberation" (p. 22). At the same time, however, Boff does not hesitate to denounce a capitalist system which exploits the poor. "It's capitalism that turns things upside down...it places things...above persons, and specifically, capital over labor" (*Feet-on-the-Ground Theology*, p. 140).

In summary, Clodovis Boff believes that the purpose of liberation theology is to articulate the cries of the oppressed, so that the church will heed that cry. He believes that an ecclesiology in tune with the times must promote an equal partnership between the pastors and the Christian base communities in nurturing and then organizing the poor and oppressed in their struggle for liberation. Boff envisages a community spirituality becoming incarnate. Here the liberator God is at work in the everyday lives of these people. "To live for liberation and a more abundant life for men and women! Is there any life that's more noble, pure and great? In this kind of service you feel a joy and happiness beyond compare. The meaning of your life is devoting your life to meaning" (*Feet-on-the-Ground Theology*, p. 163).

BOOKS

Como trabalhar com o povo: Metodologia do trabalho popular. Petrópolis, 1984.

Feet-on-the-Ground Theology: A Brazilian Journey. Maryknoll, N.Y.: Orbis Books, 1987.

Liberation Theology: From Dialogue to Confrontation. With Leonardo Boff. San Francisco: Harper & Row, 1986.

Theology and Praxis: Epistemological Foundations. Maryknoll, N.Y.: Orbis Books, 1987.

ARTICLES

"Agente de Pastoral e Povo," *Revista Eclesiástica Brasileira* 40, 1980, pp. 216-242.

"O Evangelho do Poder-Serviço," *Publicacões CRB*, Rio de Janeiro, 1984.

"O uso do 'marxismo' em teologia," *Cadernos do ISER*, May 1984.

"Retrato de 15 anos da TdL," *Revista Eclesiástica Brasileira* 46, 1986, pp. 263-271.

LEONARDO BOFF

*The resurrected Jesus is present and active in a special way
in those who in the vast ambit of history and life carry
forward his cause. This is independent of their ideological colorings or adhesion to some religion or Christian belief. Wherever people seek the good, justice, humanitarian love, solidarity, communion and understanding between
people, wherever they dedicate themselves to overcoming
their own egoism, making this world more human and fra-
ternal, and opening themselves to the normative Transcendent for their lives, there we can say, with all certainty,
that the resurrected one is present, because the cause for
which he lived, suffered, was tried and executed is being
carried forward* (Jesus Christ Liberator, p. 219).

Leonardo Boff considers one of his major contributions to liberation theology to be the development of a christology for the Latin American setting which understands Jesus to be the radical liberator of the human condition, the one who is the human being *par excellence*, the one who did not come to establish a new religion, but a new humanity. Boff contends that in the history of the Christian church two radically different types of christology have been advanced. The first begins with the divinity of Christ, the "Christ from above"; the second starts with the humanity of Christ, the "Christ from below." Boff's preference is clearly for the latter. "I follow the Franciscan school—the synoptic, Antiochene, and Scotist tradition. I find God precisely in Jesus' total, complete humanity " (*Passion of Christ, Passion of the World*, p. xii).

Leonardo Boff was born in Concórdia, Santa Catarina, Brazil, in 1938. His father was a school teacher who identified himself with the cause of the poor, including the Blacks in Concordia. Boff considers his father a decisive influence on his life in helping him see the world from the perspective of the poor and oppressed. He attended primary and secondary schools in his home town and went on to receive graduate degrees in philosophy in Curitiba (1961), in theology in Petrópolis (1965), and then a doctorate in theology from the University of Münich (1970). Ordained a Franciscan priest, he has been professor of systematic theology in Petrópolis since 1970 and advisor to the Brazilian Conference of Bishops and the Latin American Confederation of Religious.

Boff points to two experiences in particular as having a shattering impact on his life and which have been major catalysts in the development of his theology of liberation. The first has been his work as a priest over a period of several years in a Petropolis slum. There he has come in constant daily contact with persons "who simply live by competing with the swine and the vultures for what they can find in the garbage dumps." Boff has been amazed to discover that, despite these horribly inhuman conditions, these people are still able to find hope and a sense of self-worth in their Christian base communities. Here Boff can sense the real church of Jesus Christ.

A second and similar shattering experience has been Boff's frequent excursions to the diocese of Acre-Purus in the heart of the Amazon jungles where the Catholic church consists almost entirely of small base communities of believers scattered throughout the rain forests. In his hikes through this vast area to visit and minister to the poor villagers, Boff has come to a new vision of the church and what it can and should mean to the poor and oppressed. These villagers do not envision the church as a hierarchical institution. They know nothing about Vatican pronouncements or bishops' conferences or theological reflection or Marxism. For these poor people "everything is summed up in the struggle for survival: how to withstand the violence of nature, of the rain forest and the surging rivers, of wild animals and diseases. There, faith and life, God and suffering, are one."

These experiences have had a profound impact on the development of Boff's view of Jesus as the total liberator of the human condition and have given him a vision of what the church must become. They have led Boff to write his most controversial book to date: *Church, Charism and Power: Liberation Theology and the Institutional Church* (1985). In this book he develops a model for the church as the People of God, a church of and for the poor and the weak, a church of and for the dispossessed, a liberator church that identifies and shares power with the needy. Boff maintains that the traditional model of the church perpetuated by the Vatican—the hierarchical model that puts the Pope at the pinnacle of authority and the poor and powerless at the bottom—no longer makes sense to the ones at the bottom of the heap. In fact, this hierarchical view of the church "is approaching its inevitable end" (p. 57). According to Boff, the hierarchical model only perpetuates abuse and discrimination. Boff contends that "there are violations of human rights within the church itself. These are not those abuses that are the result of individual abuses of power which are temporal in nature; we refer to those that are the result of a certain way of understanding and organizing the reality of the ecclesial structure " (p. 33).

Boff's attack against the hierarchical model of the Catholic church and its penchant for abuses against the powerless was the primary reason for his summons in 1984 to appear before the Congregation for the Doctrine of the Faith at the Vatican to explain and defend his views. As a result of this hearing, in April 1985, Boff was ordered to be "silent under obedience" for a period of one year, and to make no public appearances. As it turned out—not unlike the experience of Martin Luther in exile in Wartburg—this ban was in a very real sense a boon in providing Boff extensive time for research and writing.

In his focus on the conditions of poverty and oppression suffered by the great masses of people in his country, Boff believes that it is essential to analyse the causes of the glaring social inequalities between the majority poor and the minority rich, between the oppressed and the oppressor. Boff readily admits that Marxist analysis has helped him to understand the exploitation of the poor by a capitalistic system that extols profits at the expense of people. Marxism has also helped him to explain how so often religion has become an opiate of the people, condoning a social and economic status quo, which leaves the poor powerless and does nothing to improve their lot.

Boff minces no words in his indictment of capitalism: "The basic thing is to come to the realization that the capitalist system is evil. It never produces justice, only poverty, and as far as the First and Third Worlds are concerned has never solved any of the problems that plague the poor with regard to health, housing, work, or education." But his opposition to capitalism does not make Boff a Marxist."Marxism has never been a temptation, since its use in theology is merely instrumental. I have no interest in Marx or Marxism *per se*, but only as a potential weapon for combating poverty, injustice, and as light to betray the illusion of capitalism with its mechanisms of the exploitation of workers." Liberation theology unashamedly makes use of Marxist social analysis, but the primary motive for opposing the exploitation of the poor comes from Christian resources: the Bible, tradition, and the social teachings of the church's magisterium.

It would be utterly wrong, however, to consider Leonardo Boff a prophetic activist concerned exclusively with social and economic issues. Nothing could be further from the truth. He is adamant in stressing the importance of prayer and biblical insights. Boff's book, *The Lord's Prayer: The Prayer of Integral Liberation*, develops his notion of what he calls *transparency*; the immanent and the transcendent, the human and the divine, the prophetic and the priestly, the active and the contemplative become transparent to one another and in this *transparency* they together reveal a richer and deeper reality. Boff's book, *Saint Francis: A Model for Human Liberation*, points to Francis of Assisi as the ideal—the one who, being rich, "took on the condition of the poor and became a poor man...a protest and an act of love—a *protest* against a society that expels the poor from its midst...an *act of love* because he...became one with them" (p. 76). It is this *identification with the poor* that is absolutely central for Leonardo Boff—in "praying with them, seeing their problems, immensely greater than our own, sharing their struggles, we find motives to continue to believe, and to struggle for the integral liberation of all. The theology of liberation has taught me that only in the measure that I myself am free internally and externally shall I be able to be useful in the community liberation of others. No one liberates anyone. We always liberate ourselves together."

BOOKS

Jesus Christ Liberator: A Critical Christology for Our Time. Maryknoll, N.Y. Orbis Books, 1978.

Way of the Cross: Way of Justice. Maryknoll, N.Y.: Orbis Books, 1980.

Saint Francis: A Model for Human Liberation. New York: Crossroad, 1982.

The Lord's Prayer: The Prayer of Integral Liberation. Maryknoll, N.Y.: Orbis Books, 1983.

Salvation and Liberation: In Search of a Balance Between Faith and Politics. With Clodovis Boff. Maryknoll, N.Y.: Orbis Books, 1984.

Church, Charism and Power: Liberation Theology and the Institutional Church. New York: Crossroad, 1985.

Liberation Theology: From Dialogue to Confrontation. With Clodovis Boff. San Francisco: Harper & Row, 1986.

Passion of Christ, Passion of the World. Maryknoll, N.Y.: Orbis Books, 1987.

Introducing Liberation Theology. With Clodovis Boff. Maryknoll, N.Y.: Orbis Books, 1987.

Trinity and Society. Maryknoll, N.Y.: Orbis Books, 1988.

When Theology Listens to the Poor. San Francisco: Harper & Row, 1988.

José Míguez Bonino

Is a Christian political ethics at all possible, one that will be operative in the public sphere? In this world of power, of economic relations and structures, a world that maintains its autonomy and will not yield to voluntaristic moral ideals imposed from the outside, a world in which power and freedom seem to pull in opposite directions— what can Christians say and do? How can Christianity respond to the new practice and the new conceptions of political life in the modern world? (Toward a Christian Political Ethics, p. 21).

José Míguez Bonino has made many major contributions to Third World liberation theology but one of his most important has been the espousal of a contemporary dynamic Christian political ethics. Míguez Bonino insists that in order to be faithful to Christ in today's world, one must become fully involved in the political arena. It is in the political realm that our faith must "die and be resurrected." And the basic criterion for an authentic Christian political ethic for today is that it be centered in an unequivocal commitment to the poor.

José Míguez Bonino was born in Santa Fe, Argentina, in 1924. He received his primary and secondary education in Rosario, Argentina, where his father was a shipyard foreman. Although his family did not suffer from poverty, Míguez Bonino saw and experienced first-hand the life of the poor dock workers, went to school with the workers' children, and drank "mate" with them in their tenement houses. Míguez Bonino's parents were church-going Methodists who had converted from Catholicism. The local Methodist church at that time, composed chiefly of the dock workers, the lower classes, was very socially conscious. Míguez Bonino remembers vividly discussions on social and political issues that were sponsored by his church. As he has stated: "I think that this strange mixture of working class conditions, strong piety and social awareness have remained with me—mixed and organized or disorganized in different ways at different moments—throughout all my life."

Míguez Bonino originally planned to become a physician and in fact studied medicine for two years. But while at university, he came under the influence of some non-Marxist socialist professors and as a result he himself became fully committed to social reform. It was during these years that Juan Peron came to power in Argentina; and Míguez Bonino joined the opposition forces that were advocating democratic reforms. His own interest shifted to theology. He received a licentiate in theology from the Facultad Evangelica de Teologia in 1948 and shortly thereafter was ordained to the Methodist ministry.

Míguez Bonino served parishes in Bolivia and in Mendoza and Buenos Aires in his native country. In 1952 he received a M.A. degree from Emory University. Three years later Juan Peron was overthrown with the active support of the Catholic church and the landed aristocracy. Although Míguez Bonino and his friends had great hopes for the future of Argentina—that it would finally take care of its poor—these hopes were soon dashed as one military dictatorship after another succeeded, with the support of First World economic interests, in suppressing the rights of the oppressed. As a result Míguez Bonino and his friends began to turn to the social and economic sciences to try to understand why the oppressed never seemed to emerge from poverty. "Class analysis, the theory of dependence, the studies on neo-colonialism and imperialism which Latin American sociologists were developing, became an indispensable tool to understand ourselves."

Míguez Bonino developed an intense interest in Roman Catholic biblical studies. In 1960 he received his Ph.D. degree from Union Theological Seminary; his dissertation subject was "Scripture and Tradition in Recent Catholic Thought." Owing to his special competence in Roman Catholic studies, Míguez Bonino was chosen to be an official observer for the United Methodist church at the Second Vatican Council. His contacts with Catholic theologians and church leaders have remained close and cordial through the years. In addition, he has been a member of the Commission on Faith and Order as well as the Central Committee of the World Council of Churches (WCC), and he has served as President of the WCC. He held the position of professor of theology and ethics at the Facultad Evangelica de Teologia in Argentina from 1954 to 1969; and professor of theology and ethics at the Protestant Institute for Higher Theological Education in Buenos Aires from 1970 to 1985. He has held visiting professorships in England, Costa Rica, France, and the United States.

Míguez Bonino does not point to any specific pivotal events in his life that determined his theological development. He has lived most of his life in an area of the world where hundreds of people perish every day through malnutrition, oppression and violence, and early in his life he came to realize that a neutral stance toward such evils is not a viable option. Like many other theologians of liberation, in the 1970s he came to realize that in the ongoing struggle for liberation "God has chosen sides" and, therefore, Christians must also take sides in resisting the oppressor and freeing the oppressed. The oppressors must be liberated from their thrones of power, the oppressed from their misery and marginality. And—again like so many other Third World liberation theologians—Míguez Bonino had to reassess completely his classical theological training. As we have already noted, he found that he had to begin anew from the vantage point of the social sciences in confronting the issues of poverty and oppression. As he has expressed it: "We theologians should not forget that, after all, it was the social scientists' reflections on 'dependence and liberation' which awakened us to a basic *biblical* motif" ("For Life and Against Death: A Theology That Takes Sides," p. 175).

Míguez Bonino allies himself with another basic theme of liberation theology in his contention that "theology has to stop explaining the world and to start transforming it. *Orthopraxis*, rather than orthodoxy, becomes the criterion for theology" (*Doing Theology in a Revolutionary Situation*, p. 81). He makes no secret of the fact that he is very sympathetic to Marxist social analysis. Indeed he has not hesitated to acknowledge the positive contributions that Marxist social theory has made to liberation theology. His book *Christians and Marxists: The Mutual Challenge to Revolution* is a major contribution to the Christian-Marxist dialogue. Here he states his basic thesis, namely, that "the sociological tools, the historical horizon of interpretation, the insights into the dynamics of the social process and the revolutionary ethos and program which Marxism has either received and appropriated or itself created are, however correct or reinterpreted, indispensable for revolutionary change" (p. 8).

But even though he advocates a "Christian pilgrimage to Marxism," Míguez Bonino is by no means an avowed Marxist. Quite the contrary. In recent years he has come to the conclusion that Marxism has lost much of its punch and can no longer provide the necessary stimulus for social change. To the extent that Marxism presents itself as a full and complete understanding of humanity and the greater reality of which humanity is a part, Míguez Bonino concludes that Marxism flatly contradicts the central theological claims of the Christian faith. So, whereas Míguez Bonino is willing to borrow Marxist categories, if they are useful for understanding society's ills, this is now as far as he is willing to go. For him Marxism is a complex phenomenon which operates on several levels, which he believes can be separated and distinguished and appropriated accordingly.

In taking this middle-of-the road position, Míguez Bonino subjects himself to criticism, on the one hand, from "pure" Marxists who continue to insist that Marxism stands or falls in its totality, and, on the other hand, by non-Marxists who refuse to see anything worthwhile in Marxism. Míguez Bonino does not budge from his insistence on the validity of a middle-ground position: "I have never felt attracted to Marxism as a system; neither have I felt inclined to enroll in any anti-Marxist crusade. Since my youth...I have believed that certain elements of the Marxist economic and social analyses were correct...I have found it possible to work together with Marxists and others—on questions of human rights, for instance—with clarity and mutual respect" ("For Life and Against Death," p. 176).

It is important to add here that Míguez Bonino is highly critical of the capitalist system of today's Latin America. He claims that it is riddled with failures. For him the "socialist option"— and by that phrase he means "the social appropriation of the means of production, of the political decision, and of human freedom"—presents the best possible alternative today for Christians in Latin America.

Míguez Bonino believes that one of the most serious distortions of liberation theology today is for critics to identify it in a reductionist way: to conclude that it is *only* political action or Marxist analysis or even violent revolution. To understand liberation theology we must appreciate its organic whole, its concern for all dimensions of liberation. To be sure, a full commitment to liberation calls for a political, social, and economic praxis. But that is not all. The liberation motif must express itself in worship, celebration, and fellowship. And that is why Míguez Bonino remains convinced that the achievement of this organic whole in liberation is a crucial function of the Christian community. It is this community that includes the spiritual and contemplative, as well as the political and active.

Míguez Bonino realizes that he is participating in a struggle for liberation that will never end, and which often seems only to be getting more arduous. "During the last 10 years, my life has been very deeply involved with the human rights struggle in my country. We had to see first-hand a great deal of suffering, but also incredible courage and persistence. I have become more and more convinced of the basic truth of a theology indissolubly tied to the struggles of the poor. I have equally become more and more convinced that for us this struggle has to be rooted in a deep faith. And that this struggle is not a mere fight for economic and social justice in material terms, but a struggle of love for a new way of being people."

Míguez Bonino adds that it is important for North Americans to understand that human beings all live in the same world and that their future is inextricably interwoven. The issues that are raised by the pervasive poverty and oppression in Latin America are also issues for North Americans to address. The powers and principalities that are part of the North American scene are even more ferocious in the southern hemisphere. The solution to these problems, Míguez Bonino testifies, is to be found in the resurrection of Jesus Christ. Jesus has come into this world "not to cancel out the cross, not to insure a visible victory, but rather to confirm Jesus' practice of love and justice....The power of death is not magically suspended, but the praxis of vicarious love ("laying down our life for the brethren") through death reaches its final consummation" (*Toward a Christian Political Ethics*, p. 115).

BOOKS

Doing Theology in a Revolutionary Situation. Philadelphia: Fortress Press, 1975.

Christians and Marxists: The Mutual Challenge to Revolution. Grand Rapids, Michigan: Wm. B. Eerdmans, 1976.

Room to Be People: An Interpretation of the Message of the Bible for Today's World. Philadelphia: Fortress Press, 1979.

Toward a Christian Political Ethics. Philadelphia: Fortress Press, 1983.

Faces of Jesus. Edited by Jose' Míguez Bonino. Maryknoll, N.Y.: Orbis Books, 1984.

ARTICLES

"How Does God Act in History?" *Christ and the Younger Churches*. Edited by José Míguez Bonino. London: SPCK, 1972, pp. 21-32.

"For Life and Against Death: A Theology That Takes Sides." *Theologies in Transition*. Edited by James M. Wall. New York: Crossroad, 1981.

"Ecumenical Sharing in a World of Imbalance: A Latin American Perspective." *China Notes*, Vol. 24, Nos. 2, 3, Spring and Summer 1986, pp. 377-380.

"The Biblical Roots of Justice," *Word and World: Theology for Christian Ministry*, Vol. 12, No. 1, Winter 1987, pp. 12-22.

ERNESTO CARDENAL

I have become politicized by the contemplative life. Meditation is what brought me to political radicalization. I came to the revolution by way of the Gospels. It was not by reading Marx but Christ. It can be said that the Gospels made me a Marxist (Flights of Victory, p. xv).

Ernesto Cardenal the poet has become Ernesto Cardenal the radical politician. His chief contribution to liberation theology has been to combine the roles of poet and politician within a Christian perspective. To consider Cardenal only as a member of the Nicaraguan government is to distort both his poetic gifts and his deeply-held Christian faith.

Ernesto Cardenal was born in Granada, Nicaragua, in 1925. After finishing high school in his home town, he studied literature at the University of Managua and in 1946 received a licentiate in philosophy and letters from the National Autonomous University of Mexico. From his earliest years Cardenal took a special interest in writing poetry. His studies at the University of Mexico culminated in his dissertation on Nicaraguan poetry. In the late 1940s, he continued his studies in literature at Columbia University in New York City, and he also took a year to travel throughout western Europe. He returned to his native country in 1950, where he became friendly with a group of people who were opposed to the dictatorship of Anastasio Somoza Garcia, who had been in power since 1936. But poetry remained Cardenal's first love, and during the 1940s and 1950s, his poems appeared regularly in print.

In 1957 Cardenal became a novice in the Trappist monastery of Our Lady of Gethsemene in Kentucky, where the poet-priest Thomas Merton became his mentor. Two years later because of poor health, Cardenal left the monastic life. He took up the study of theology in Cuernavaca, Mexico. He also spent a period of time studying theology in Colombia where he came to know and admire Camilo Torres, the Colombian priest, who joined a guerilla force and was slain in 1966. It was during his stay in Colombia that Cardenal came in contact with the early stirrings of liberation theology rooted in the emerging Christian base communities.

Ernesto Cardenal was ordained a priest in Managua in 1964. Within a year he and two of his close friends, William Agudelo and Carlos Alberto, had founded a small Christian community in the archipelago of Solentiname, a group of small islands in Lake Nicaragua. From 1965 to 1977, Cardenal lived, worked, studied the Bible, and prayed with the several hundred fisher folk, patterning his ministry after the teachings of his former tutor, Thomas Merton. Each Sunday the community would come together in their church, named Our Lady of Solentiname, to study the Scripture and relate its teachings to their everyday lives. Many of these dialogues have been preserved in a four-volume work, *The*

Gospel in Solentiname, a rich first-hand account of the life and ministry of a Christian base community. During these years, Cardenal was able to combine his religious, poetic, and political interests, and all three dimensions have remained important to him throughout his life, a combination that has been his distinctive contribution to liberation theology.

Although Cardenal had been committed to change through nonviolence, he began to re-examine that stance after a trip to Cuba in 1970, where he served as a judge in a poetry contest. There he glimpsed the possibility of building a society in Nicaragua that would be far more just and humane than the brutal dictatorship under Somoza. In the early and middle 1970s, Cardenal became more active in the struggle against Somoza, and gradually the Solentiname community became a bastion of support for the guerilla activities of the Sandinistas who were opposing the government. In 1977 many of the members of the Solentiname community joined in an attack on Somoza's National Guard in the town of San Carlos on the border of Costa Rica. After an abortive victory, the Solentiname community was forced to abandon their homes and flee for their lives in the face of invading military forces from the National Guard. The community's buildings were all destroyed, except for the church, which Somoza's forces used as an army barracks. Later, in one of his poems Ernesto Cardenal wrote of his experiences in flying over the ruined Solentiname compound:

> First came the lake, calm. And in it
> my place, what was my home, Solentiname.
> All the islands grouped together; they seemed just like
> one.
> But I could distinguish them one by one from afar, say
> their name.
> The point where our community was. Everything demo-
> lished.
> The library burned. That hammock under a roof of palms
> with the lake in front.
> Elvis and his guitar. Where did the guardsmen bury
> them?...
> No one else has seen a thing...And the stewardesses
> start serving plastic food as if nothing's happened.
> (*Flights of Victory,* pp. 19-21.)

After the Solentiname exile Cardenal became a more active participant in the Sandinista revolution. He traveled throughout the United States, Europe, and Latin America, raising money to support the Sandinistan cause. When the Sandinistas became victorious over Somoza's forces in 1979, Cardenal returned to Managua where he became Minister of Culture in the new government. In this capacity, Cardenal's primary aim has been to "democratize culture," to encourage the Nicaraguan people—especially the poor—to develop and appreciate their own distinctive heritage. He has built cultural houses and has directed programs in literature, poetry, art, and music to enable the people to experience the richness of their own traditions.

Cardenal insists that he "came to the revolution by way of the Gospels." One finds confirmation of his contention in the Solentiname dialogues, which predate his involvement in the Sandinista revolution. Here one finds these passages: "God is showing us with this Gospel that the rich think of us as dirt"; "Jesus came to share the lot of the poor"; "The Gospel was what radicalized us politically" (vol. 1, pp. 49, 47, 268). Cardenal himself believes that his most important contribution to liberation theology has been the publication of *The Gospel in Solentiname*, which illustrates how theology can and should emerge "from below" out of the lives of Christian base communities as they reflect on the meaning of the Gospel.

To be sure, since the destruction of the Solentiname compound, Cardenal has reluctantly come to see the need to meet violence with violence. But he insists that the Sandinistas, for example, did not introduce violence into Nicaraguan society. Violence was already there, institutionalized in the social order that divided oppressor from oppressed and rich from poor—and which became personalized in the National Guard's harsh, brutal treatment of its opponents. Cardenal admits that he has incorporated Marxism into his theology. As he puts it: "Marxism plays in our theology the role that Aristotelianism had in that of Saint Thomas Aquinas." Cardenal believes that the most important theological issue facing liberation theologians today is how to defend themselves against persecution from the official church and from the secular authorities of many countries. These church and secular leaders too often confuse liberation theology with communism which in itself, he says, "would not be a bad thing if it weren't for the fact that 'communism' is thought of as something Satanic."

Cardenal's life and work seeks to witness to the love of God through the medium of poetry. And like so many other liberation theologians, he sees idolatry as a major menace. "True atheism, the true denial of God, for me is Esso, Standard Oil, and the Dow Chemical Company, which makes profits by manufacturing napalm. This is the true denial of God" (Jose Arguella, "Cardenal's Theo-poetry," *Christianity and Crisis*, April 1985, pp. 141-143). In his recent book, *Flights of Victory*, Ernesto Cardenal shows his gifts as one of the leading poets of Latin America, a poet become prophet. Describing the face of liberated Nicaragua, he writes:

> To live without exploitation's hatred.
> To love each other in a lovely land
> very lovely, not only for the land
> but for its people
> above all for its people.
> That's why God rendered it so lovely (p. 123).

BOOKS

To Live Is to Love. New York: Herder and Herder, 1972.

In Cuba. New York: New Directions, 1974.

Hora O. New York: New Directions, 1975.

Apocalypse and Other Poems. New York: New Directions, 1977.

Homage to the American Indian. Ann Arbor: UMI Research Press, 1973.

Psalms. New York: Crossroad, 1981.

The Gospel in Solentiname. Maryknoll, N.Y.: Orbis Books, 1976-1982.

With Walker in Nicaragua and Other Early Poems. Middletown, Conn.: Wesleyan University Press, 1985.

Flights of Victory/Vuelos de Victoria. Maryknoll, N.Y.: Orbis Books, 1985.

JOSÉ COMBLIN

The salvation of Jesus Christ is mystical and political at the same time. It is political because we live enslaved to oppressive structures from which we must free ourselves in order to establish justice. It is mystical because the effort would turn into another form of oppression if it were not motivated by, and suffused with, human freedom and love (The Meaning of Mission, p. 60).

The political and the mystical: these are the two essential ingredients in the life and writings of José Comblin. In *The Church and the National Security State*, Comblin writes of the need for a theology of revolution to confront the U.S.-supported national security system, which now dominates most Latin American nations and seeks to conquer the rest of Latin America in the near future. He maintains that changing the structures of society is imperative if the poor and oppressed are to achieve liberation. In *The Meaning of Mission*, Comblin adds that such structural change will be of no avail unless individuals themselves are saved. Structural change that is achieved by sinful human beings will only produce new structures of domination and oppression. Thus, for Comblin the prophetic and the mystical, justice and love must always balance one another.

José Comblin was born in Brussels, Belgium, in 1923, where he was raised in a strong Catholic environment. He was ordained a priest in 1947 and received a Ph.D. in theology in 1950 from the University of Louvain. At Louvain he specialized in New Testament studies and was thoroughly immersed in the two cultures of Latin rationalism and German romanticism, which both strongly influenced his theological development. From 1947 until 1958, he served parishes in Brussels. But then he responded to an appeal by Pope Pius XII to the Catholics of the First World during the mid-1950s. The pope asked for volunteers to defend Latin America from the inroads of communism. Accordingly, Comblin went to Campinas in the state of São Paulo, Brazil. He taught in the seminary there and served as adviser to Catholic Action groups. Comblin was professor of theology in the Catholic University of Santiago, Chile, from 1962 to 1964; and he served as professor of theology in the regional seminary in Recife, Brazil, from 1965 to 1972.

During these years he came under the influence of Dom Helder Camara and he was introduced to a new world, a world teeming with poverty. As a result, his entire attitude toward both church and society underwent a profound change. He came to know and participate in the struggles of the oppressed people, the mestizos, the blacks and Amerindians. He became more outspoken against the oppressive Brazilian government in the process. Comblin also came to see the United States, not as the great liberator, a view which he had held during his years in Belgium, but as the ruthless oppressor allied with Latin American military governments. Archbishop Helder Camara remembers Comblin as a prime living example of the committed theologian always up-to-date in scholarly pursuits, yet increasingly committed to an authentic flesh-and-blood theology emerging from the lives of the poor and oppressed. In 1972, however, Comblin was expelled from Brazil for his "subversive activities" and from 1972 to 1980 he taught theology at the Catholic University in Talco, Chile, as well as at Louvain. He presently works as a parish priest in João Pessoa in Brazil, although he travels frequently throughout most of Latin America and teaches part-time at Louvain.

For Comblin, it is not possible to divorce Latin American liberation theology from the political arena. His thirty years of living with the oppressed peoples in twenty nations has convinced him that "the experience of the poor is the starting point of a true knowledge of Christianity," and that the real theologians in Latin America "are not professors, but militants" whose commitment to liberation cannot be distinguished from their intellectual life (*The Church and the National Security State,* pp. *xii,* 6). Comblin believes that Vatican II and recent social encyclicals have had a deep impact on Latin America and are important factors in the emergence of liberation theology.

Comblin is insistent that liberation must be applied to all areas of personal and social life. For him this includes "movements to liberate persons from society's laws, structures and obligations; movements to liberate women from the masculine bias of society as a whole; movements to liberate youth from a society developed in terms of its adult citizens; movements to liberate sex from personal and social taboos; movements to liberate workers from a society established in terms of productivity as defined by the interests of the dominating class; movements to liberate colonized and dominated peoples from an international order founded in terms of the privileges of the more powerful nations" (p. 121). In short, the human demand for liberation has never been as extensive as it is today.

Still, Comblin is pessimistic about the possibility that these goals of liberation will be achieved. For one thing the military dictatorships in Latin America have become more ruthless in their suppression of the oppressed. Then, too, the emergence of liberation theology has provoked a backlash from the "new right" in both politics and religion, which stresses a personal soul-saving faith and espouses a right wing political agenda. Comblin sees little hope that what he calls the "ecclesiastical apparatchiks" will side with the poor. In fact, he says that the various church hierarchies are almost universally connected with each nation's dominant political power structure. Even the Pope will always search for an accommodation with the President of the United States and with the established political and economic systems all over the world. Consequently, the Catholic church, precisely because of its entrenched identification with the world's principalities and powers, will never be able to imitate Jesus' way of life. Liberation movements will inevitably remain minority enclaves. Liberation theology itself has entered a profound state of crisis for survival that may give birth to a new strategy, even a new name, perhaps a "theology of captivity."

In recent years Comblin has become convinced that Marxism is unavoidable in the Third World. It has become an indispensable tool to justify liberation movements. There simply seems to be no other alternative tool of analysis that works. But Comblin is quick to point out that there are many types of Marxism, and that Third World peoples utilize Marxism for their present social needs without adopting the entire Marxist ideology. Comblin himself sees many weaknesses in Marxist ideology, especially in its denial of freedom. And this same Marxist ideology, which expels freedom from history, also expels God from humankind and history.

Comblin believes that the future of Christianity in Latin America lies in a renewed search for liberating styles of life that will lead to a more humane and just civilization. This willingness to break out of the old molds and identify with reform movements always runs the risk of promoting and abetting violence, but far better to face this risk than to retreat into numbing inaction. In their constant and continuing struggles for liberation, the poor peoples of the Third World retain a strong dimension of hope. They want to believe that new societies can be created in which there are no masters and slaves, rich and poor, intellectuals and illiterates. They must, says Comblin, live as pilgrims who can abandon their old homes if necessary and "walk toward other homes in the midst of the desert."

But in this pilgrimage, which will inevitably involve the complete transformation of the political and social system, Comblin reminds us that we must always be mindful of the mystical component, that salvation begins in the individual human heart, that in the final analysis it is in Jesus Christ that we find a new way of being truly human. "No structures can provide love unless there are human beings around who are willing to show love" (*The Meaning of Mission*, p. 71).

BOOKS

Jesus of Nazareth: Meditations on His Humanity. Maryknoll, N.Y.: Orbis Books, 1976.

The Meaning of Mission: Jesus, Christians and the Wayfaring Church. Maryknoll, N.Y.: Orbis Books, 1977.

Sent from the Father: Meditations on the Fourth Gospel. Maryknoll, N.Y.: Orbis Books, 1979.

The Church and the National Security State. Maryknoll, N.Y.: Orbis Books, 1979.

Cry of the Oppressed, Cry of Jesus: Meditations on Scripture and Contemporary Struggle. Maryknoll, N.Y.: Orbis Books, 1988.

ENRIQUE DUSSEL

The oppressed are the poor *in political terms (person, class, nation), the* woman *in the macho sexual system, the child, youth, the* people *in the pedagogy of cultural domination. All the problems and topics of logic, philosophy of language, anthropology, and metaphysics acquire new light and new meaning when viewed from the absolute and nevertheless concrete (the opposite of universal) criterion that philosophy is the weapon of the liberation of the oppressed* (Philosophy of Liberation, *p. 189).*

Enrique Dussel can be counted among the early generation of Latin American liberation theologians whose writings have had a powerful impact in setting the agenda for the rapid spread of Latin American liberation theology. His book, *History of the Church in Latin America: Colonialism to Liberation (1492-1979)* (which first appeared in English as a third edition in 1981), was originally published in 1967 in Spanish. It was the first one-volume history of the church in Latin America, and was widely read by other first-generation liberation theologians including Gustavo Gutiérrez. Dussel's five volume work, *Filosofia Etica Latinomericana* (1970-1975), was also the original attempt to provide a philosophical basis for a liberation ethic. His more than thirty books have continued to build on his basic premise that "philosophy is the weapon of the liberation of the oppressed."

Enrique Dussel was born in La Paz in the desert of Mendoza, Argentina, in 1934. His father was a physician who spent much of his time caring for the farmers and the poor in and around Mendoza, thereby instilling in Enrique a sensitivity to the plight of the poor. His mother was a devout Catholic who played the key role in nurturing her son's faith. From the age of eight through early manhood, Dussel participated in Catholic Action movements. He showed a special interest in the subjects of philosophy and theology, and received a licentiate in philosophy from the Universidad Nacional del Cuyo in Mendoza in 1957. At the university he served as President of the Young Christian Student Movement (JEC).

Dussel then traveled to Europe for his graduate studies. He earned a doctorate in philosophy at the Universidad Central de Madrid in 1959. This period spent in Spain coincided with the struggles of the Spanish poor against the brutality of the forces of General Francisco Franco. Dussel's increasing sensitivity to poverty and oppression led him to identify with the anti-Franco supporters. For the next two years he lived in Israel, a crucial period of his life to which we shall return. In 1961 he moved to Paris to study at the Sorbonne. He spent two years in Germany, studying under, among others, Joseph Ratzinger in Münster. He returned to Paris where he received a licentiate in theology from the Institut Catholique de Paris in 1965 and a doctorate in history from the Sorbonne in 1967, specializing in the history of the church in Latin America, the subject of his book. In 1981, he received an honorary doctorate in theology in Freiburg, Switzerland.

Enrique Dussel singles out the years 1959 to 1961 when he lived in Israel as a decisive turning point in his life. During this period he worked both as a fisherman and as a carpenter and lived with a small community of Christians, which included Paul Gauthier, in an Arab construction cooperative. Together the members of this Christian base community would read the Bible, focusing especially on the gospels, and they would relate the biblical teachings to their everyday lives. Every Saturday morning Dussel and other members of the community would go to the local synagogue with the express purpose of reading from the book of Isaiah, as Jesus had done: "And he came to Nazareth, where he had been brought up; and he went to the synagogue, as his custom was, on the sabbath day. And he stood up to read; and there was given to him the book of the prophet Isaiah. He opened the book and found the place where it was written, 'The Spirit of the Lord is upon me, because he has anointed me to preach good news to the poor' " (Luke 4:14-18). This particular passage—one singled out by so many Third World liberation theologians—constitutes for Dussel the essence of the Christian gospel.

This period witnessed Dussel's conversion to a new life and a new vocation. Dussel and Paul Gauthier often discussed how Jesus had identified himself with the poor. In 1962 Gauthier published his booklet, *The Poor, Jesus and the Church*. Dussel himself began to develop the theme of "the poor one," which has become a major topic in his writings. Indeed Dussel claims: "I think I am the first liberation theologian to have discovered this theme (not only *poverty*, but the *poor one*)." Here Dussel stresses the importance of seeing the poor as "other," as "people" who themselves are the subjects of the Kingdom.

Dussel returned to Latin America in 1967, where he taught at the Pastoral Institute of Latin America in Quito, Ecuador, the Universidad Nacional de Resistencia in Chaco, Argentina, and from 1968 to 1975 at the Universidad Nacional del Cuyo in his home town of Mendoza. Exiled as a political refugee from his native country, Dussel has been professor of ethics at the Universidad Nacional Autónoma de Mexico in Mexico City since 1976. He also serves as President of the Commission on the Study of the History of Latin America and is supervising the Commission in its projected ten-volume series on Latin American church history.

For the past decade, Dussel has concentrated on providing a philosophical and historical framework for liberation theology. He wants North Americans to understand that the theology of liberation constitutes a major epistemological shift, which demands a total rethinking of how theology is done. He asks: "Is it possible to philosophize authentically in a dependent and dominated culture? Is a Latin American philosophy possible?" (*Philosophy of Liberation*, p. 172). And he answers: "*To think of everything in the light of the provocative word of the people*—the poor, the castrated woman, the child, the culturally dominated youth, the aged person discarded by the consumer society— shouldering infinite responsibility and in the presence of the Infinite is philosophy of liberation" (p. 178). To think theologically, Dussel insists, is to "reflect on the Christian day-to-dayness" (*Ethics and the Theology of Liberation*, p. 173).

Dussel admits that until 1975 his knowledge of Marxism was peripheral. He still maintains that he has made no major use of Marxist thought. During his years of exile in Mexico, however, he has studied and written extensively about Marxism. Dussel believes that Marx's analysis of society's inequities is surely pertinent, but Marx's most serious mistake was his refusal to affirm the "God-other." Consequently, Marxism has no transcendent principle that can serve as a radical critique and judgment on all human systems.

Like his Third World liberation colleagues, Dussel insists that liberation theology must emerge from the spiritual experience of the poor, from their daily bible reading, a discipline that became so indispensable for Dussel himself during his years in Israel. "When the oppressed who struggle against the death that the system allots to them begin, through the praxis of liberation, the struggle for life, novelty irrupts in history beyond the Being of the system. A new philosophy, a positive one, necessarily makes its appearance. The novelty is not originally and primarily philosophical; it is originally and primarily historical and real; it is the liberation of the oppressed" (*Philosophy of Liberation*, p. 189).

Another theme to which Dussel has devoted increasing attention is that of *sacramentality*. He wants to develop a sacramental community ethic for the lives of the masses of "poor ones" in Latin America. Here the eucharist becomes "the sacrament of anticipation of the kingdom to come, but kingdom understood as the end to all oppression and, therefore, sin" (*Ethics and the Theology of Liberation*, p. 99).

Dussel envisions liberation theology as valid for the entire world and not only for the Third World. He maintains that the

Christians of the Third World today have a unique responsibility to remind their mother churches in the West of the basic liberating message of the Christian faith. In Dussel's words: "We are at the end of the 'missionary age' and at the beginning of that of 'solidarity' among 'local churches'....Now Rome learns from Latin America, Geneva from Africa, New York from the Philippines or China. It is *the age of a new universality* ("The Ebb and Flow of the Gospel," p. 95).

BOOKS

History and the Theology of Liberation. Maryknoll, N.Y.: Orbis Books, 1976.

Ethics and the Theology of Liberation. Maryknoll, N.Y.: Orbis Books, 1978.

A History of the Church in Latin America: Colonialism to Liberation, 1492-1979. Grand Rapids, Michigan: Wm. B. Eerdmans, 1981.

Philosophy of Liberation. Maryknoll, N.Y.: Orbis Books, 1985.

Ethics and Community. Maryknoll, N.Y.: Orbis Books, 1988.

ARTICLES

"The Bread of the Eucharist Celebration," *Can We Always Celebrate the Eucharist?* Edited by Mary Collins and David Power. Edinburgh: T. and T. Clark Ltd., 1982, pp. 56-65.

" 'Populus Dei' in Populo Pauperium: From Vatican II to Medellin and Puebla," *The People of God Amidst the Poor.* Edited by Leonardo Boff and Virgilio Elizondo. Edinburgh: T. and T. Clark Ltd, 1984, pp. 35-44.

"The Ebb and Flow of the Gospel," *Option for the Poor: Challenge to the Rich Countries.* Edited by Leonardo Boff and Virgilio Elizondo. Edinburgh: T. and T. Clark Ltd, 1986, pp. 91-100.

SEGUNDO GALILEA

The raison d'être of the theology of liberation is not to be sought in its sociological critique, nor in its analyses of dependency and underdevelopment, nor in political ideologies, however useful or even necessary all these things may be for the implementation of justice. The raison d'etre of the theology of liberation is to be sought in the very nature of the Christian God, as preached by Jesus Christ and conveyed to humankind by his church today (The Beatitudes, pp. 19-20).

Segundo Galilea is a vigorous advocate of a spirituality of liberation. He believes that the primary challenge to the faith of contemporary Christians is to find Jesus Christ in the very depths of the realities that surround us in our everyday world. Born in Santiago, Chile, in 1928, Segundo Galilea received a licentiate in theology in Santiago and was ordained to the priesthood in 1956. His first years as a priest were spent working among the poor in the slums of his home town. He served as Director of the Pastoral Review in Santiago, 1958-1962; he was Director of CELAM's Latin American Pastoral Institute, 1964-1974, and theological consultant to the Latin American Religious Conference, 1975-1984. Since 1982, he has been theological consultant to the United States Hispanic Apostolate, and since 1983, consultant to CELAM's Mission Department.

From the beginning of his ministry, Segundo Galilea has been interested in the formation of a Christian spirituality—a spirituality that would fit the lives of the poor people in his country. Strongly influenced by the writings of Charles de Foucauld, Galilea focused on a spirituality of the poor long before he had even heard of liberation theology. It was during his years as Director of the Latin American Pastoral Institute, that he began to see the need for a theological undergirding for his developing concern for Christian spirituality. His rediscovery of the sixteenth-century Spanish mystic John of the Cross was an important element in his growing appreciation of the crucial link between spirituality and theology.

In his book, *Following Jesus*, Galilea intertwines the dimensions of contemplation and action, of service to the world and the worship of God. The whole point of the life of prayer consists in "going out of oneself in order to meet the Other." Galilea is critical of the "committed militants" who over-stress the social, economic, and political aspects of liberation. But he is equally critical of the "religious contemplatives" who focus too much on the interior life at the expense of the social dimension. For Galilea, an authentic Christian spirituality "brings about the synthesis of the militant and the mystic, of the politician and the contemplative, overcoming the false contradiction between the 'contemplative-religious' and the 'committed-militant' " (*Following Jesus*, p. 63).

Galilea is well aware of the danger of politicizing the evangelical mission of the church, an abuse which he recognizes in some forms of liberation theology. And he strongly opposes what he considers the inadequacy of many radical or overly intellectual formulations of some of the developments in liberation theology. But such extremes should never detract from the mandate to liberate the poor and needy from social-economic-political oppression. "Pastoral activity should never lose its socio-political challenge, which is part of its very essence" (p. 105).

Galilea finds in the life and ministry of Jesus the model for an authentic spirituality. Jesus is the complete liberator—and a dangerous liberator if we take him seriously. Jesus challenges the political structures which keep the poor oppressed. "For the *system* Jesus is more dangerous than a revolutionary and his message is more subversive than a political proclamation" (p. 108). To ignore the *political* dimension of Jesus' ministry is to ignore the true meaning that Jesus' understanding of liberation has for the "little ones" of history.

Segundo Galilea's writings resonate with the twin components of contemplation and action as essential for Christian spirituality. For him the essence of a theology of liberation is a new way to evangelize, a way in which the poor and oppressed achieve "integral liberation" rooted in the everyday lives of their own indigenous basic Christian communities. He readily admits that some earlier forms of liberation theology had a misplaced confidence in the role of revolutionary struggle and put too much emphasis on the plight of the poor at the expense of other levels of society that also need liberation. He sees the need today for a growing sensitivity within all social classes, a spirituality that encompasses all people.

In his critique of the causes of social inequality, Galilea has never been attracted by Marxist philosophy, or even by Marxist social analysis. Indeed he is critical of all ideologies and forms of analysis that seem to have the answers all locked up. He has serious misgivings about borrowing either Marxist or capitalist social analysis, lock, stock and barrel. He is wary of what he calls "secularized western modernity" whose "isms" claim to have the panacea for Latin America's problems. Latin American problems, he insists, must have Latin American solutions.

In the 1980s, Segundo Galilea's dominant concern for the emergence of a spirituality encompassing all people has taken a new direction in his encounter with the Far East, with Asian Christians, and with the peoples of non-Christian religions. As a result of this encounter, he now speaks of a plurality of spiritualities that derive from a rich variety of cultural and religious backgrounds. He has begun to see the West—including his own Latin America—from the "outside." He has become more painfully aware of the inherent limitations of many current forms of "Western" liberation theology and spirituality. He now finds himself more critical of his previous circumscribed Latin American worldview and is groping for a new synthesis of different manifestations of spirituality that will encompass an authentic Christian faithstance, yet will include the positive ingredients to be found in the religious traditions of India and other Far Eastern countries.

In his ministry and his writings, Segundo Galilea represents the perfect rejoinder to those critics who predict that liberation theology will itself become a rigid, unchanging system. He remains open and responsive to changing situations and experiences which, in their deepest stirrings, are in harmony with what he believes to be the ultimate purpose and motivation of human life which is God.

BOOKS

Following Jesus. Maryknoll, N.Y.: Orbis Books, 1981.

The Beatitudes: To Evangelize as Jesus Did. Maryknoll, N.Y.: Orbis Books, 1984.

The Future of Our Past: The Spanish Mystics Speak to Contemporary Spirituality. Notre Dame, Indiana: Ave Maria, 1985.

Espiritualidad de la Esperanza. Madrid: Ediciones Paulinas, 1987.

The Way of Living Faith: A Spirituality of Liberation. San Francisco: Harper & Row, 1988.

ARTICLES

"Liberation as an Encounter with Politics and Contemplation," *The Mystical and Political Dimensions of the Christian Faith.* Edited by Claude Geffré and Gustavo Gutiérrez. New York: Seabury, 1974, pp. 19-34.

"Between Medellín and Puebla," *Cross Currents,* Vol. 28, No. 1, Spring 1978, pp. 71-79.

"Liberation Theology and New Tasks Facing Christians," *Frontiers of Theology in Latin America.* Edited by Rosino Gibellini. Maryknoll, N.Y.: Orbis Books, 1979, pp. 163-184.

"Between India and New York," *Commonweal,* Vol. 107, No. 3, February 8, 1985, pp. 202-203.

"Spirituality of Liberation," *Word,* Vol. 25, No. 3, July 1985, pp. 186-194.

GUSTAVO GUTIÉRREZ

Liberation is an all-embracing process that leaves no dimension of human life untouched, because when all is said and done it expresses the saving action of God in history (We Drink from Our Own Wells, *p. 2).*

Gustavo Gutiérrez of Peru is without question the pre-eminent Third World liberation theologian. The year 1988 marks the fifteenth anniversary of the English translation of his epoch-making book, *A Theology of Liberation*. The quotation above contains the two aspects of liberation theology that Gutiérrez considers essential: liberation as an all-embracing process encompassing the total life of the individual, and society *and* liberation centered in God as savior in history.

Gustavo Gutiérrez was born in Lima, Peru, in 1928. He experienced discrimination at an early age because of his mestizo blood, and he also experienced poverty. During childhood he suffered from osteomyelitis, which kept him bedridden for six years and left him with a permanent limp. Gutiérrez, who originally intended to become a doctor, studied medicine at San Marcos University in Lima and received a degree in medical science. During these same years he studied the writings of Karl Marx and joined student Christian movements that were protesting social and economic inequalities in Peruvian society. Later his interests turned toward psychiatry, and for a time he studied philosophy at the Catholic University in Lima. Gradually his interests gravitated toward theology and the priesthood. After completing theological studies in Santiago, Chile, he received degrees in philosophy and psychology from Louvain; and, in 1959, he earned a Ph.D. in theology at the University of Lyon, France. At both European institutions he continued his studies of Karl Marx. He was ordained a priest in 1959 and studied that year at the Gregorian University in Rome.

Gutiérrez returned to his native country in the early 1960s where he became a pastor at a parish in Lima, an instructor in the department of theology and social sciences at the Catholic University of Lima, and chaplain to the National Union of Catholic Students. His exposure to the poor people of his parish in Lima challenged the traditional theological education he had received in Europe. He became involved in some of the basic Christian communities that were taking root in Peru in the early 1960s. During this same period, he came under the influence of two "radicals," "Che" Guevara, his fellow student at Louvain, and Camilo Torres. Both were members of the opposition forces in Bolivia and Colombia respectively, and both were martyred for their political activities. Because he identified himself with the poor people of Lima, Gutiérrez moved to a small apartment in the slums of Rimac, one of the most impoverished areas of Lima.

By the late 1960s Gutiérrez had begun to articulate a theology of liberation in which he sought to express the hopes and needs of the poor and oppressed peoples in their yearnings for freedom, justice, and dignity. At the Medellín, Colombia, conference of Latin American bishops (CELAM II) in 1968, he served as a theological advisor, calling attention to the plight of the poor and the challenge for the Christian faith to confront their suffering head-on by showing "a preferential option for the poor."

Gutiérrez singles out the year 1968 as the pivotal year for the birth of Latin American liberation theology. Since that year he has come to increasing prominence as the primary spokesperson for liberation theology. His *A Theology of Liberation* has attracted a wide readership in the English-speaking world and has been translated into more than ten languages. He participated in the "Christians for Socialism" Conference in Chile in 1973, addressed the conference on "Theology in the Americas" in Detroit in 1975, and was a visiting professor at Union Theological Seminary in 1976-77. Since 1978, he has been a regular visitor to the United States, serving as visiting professor and speaking at numerous conferences. Although the hierarchy of the Catholic church has sought to downplay his influence, e.g. he was shut out of the official proceedings of the conference of Latin American bishops (CELAM III) in Puebla, Mexico, in 1979, he has never been officially silenced by the magisterium. (A Vatican commission was sent to Peru in 1983 to investigate his orthodoxy.) Gutiérrez maintains that his own Christian witness has been deepened through his rediscovery of Bartolomé de Las Casas, the sixteenth century Spanish liberator-priest who sided with the natives of Santo Domingo in their struggles against the Spanish invaders. And in the 1960s, the late Peruvian novelist José María Arguedas helped Gutiérrez understand how different are the gods of the powerful and the poor. Gutiérrez dedicated *A Theology of Liberation* to Arguedas.

It is important to remember that, for Gutiérrez, liberation is not confined to the socio-economic-political dimension. Even in his first book, *A Theology of Liberation*, Gutiérrez includes a section on "A Spirituality of Liberation," a theme that he expands upon in *We Drink from Our Own Wells*. Here he underscores liberation as an all-embracing process, a spirituality that is "a walking in freedom according to the Spirit of love and life" (p. 35). Gutiérrez sees a vital connection between contemplation and action, between theology and spirituality. In his book, *On Job: God-talk and the*

Suffering of the Innocent, he writes of the need for two different kinds of languages—the prophetic and the contemplative—which, though different, must be fully integrated into one's faith. "Mystical language expresses the gratuitousness of God's love; prophetic language expresses the demands this love makes....Both languages are necessary and therefore indispensable; they also feed and correct each other" (p. 95).

Through the years Gutiérrez has not hesitated to use Marxist social analysis in his effort to understand the plight of the poor. After all, he maintains, social science is a necessary discipline for investigating society's problems; and one should be willing to use Marxist insights in the same way that Freudian insights are used in contemporary psychology. But Gutiérrez is very definitely not a Marxist. His over-riding concern is to confront, to understand, to sympathize with the stuggles for justice and liberation of the poor peoples of Latin America and to place before all Christians Jesus' words: "God has anointed me to preach good news to the poor...to set at liberty those who are oppressed."

In short, for Gustavo Gutiérrez the whole point of a theology of liberation is to discern "the irruption of the poor" in today's world from the perspective of the Christian faith; to deepen the hopes of the suffering; to strengthen the popular religiosity of the poor; and to proclaim the demands of the Gospel in achieving liberation for the poor. Gutiérrez believes that liberation theology today must be equally concerned with the feminine and racial dimensions of oppression. But it must never reduce the evangelical message to politics and social issues. Liberation theology attempts to speak about God from the underside of history. And this new understanding of theology or, better still, spirituality, must be a community enterprise: "It is the passage of a people through the solitude and dangers of the desert, as it carves out its own way in the following of Jesus Christ. This spiritual experience is the well from which we must drink. From it we draw the promise of resurrection" (*We Drink from Our Own Wells,* p. 137).

BOOKS

A Theology of Liberation. Maryknoll, N.Y.: Orbis Books, 1973.

The Mystical and Political Dimensions of the Christian Faith. Edited by Gustavo Gutiérrez and Claude Geffre. New York: Herder and Herder, 1974.

Liberation and Change. Edited by Gustavo Gutiérrez and Richard Shaull. Atlanta: John Knox Press, 1977.

The Power of the Poor in History. Maryknoll, N.Y.: Orbis Books, 1983.

We Drink from Our Own Wells. Maryknoll, N.Y.: Orbis Books, 1984.

Different Theologies: Common Responsibility. Edited by Gustavo Gutiérrez, Claude Geffre and Virgilio Elizondo. Edinburgh: T. and T. Clark, 1984.

On Job: God-talk and the Suffering of the Innocent. Maryknoll, N.Y.: Orbis Books, 1987.

João Batista Libanio

Spiritual discernment is an ascetic practice that seeks to discover the will of God—that is, a way of incorporating love, concrete charity, into our lives. We can say without equivocation that social justice is one of the more privileged works—mediations—of charity. And politics is in turn the privileged field for the realization of justice. Thus it would seem that politics is a privileged field for discernment (Spiritual Discernment and Politics, *p. 2*).

João Batista Libanio seeks to integrate faith and politics in a way that will create a spirituality of liberation centered in God that emerges from the everyday lives of the poor and oppressed. Libanio was born in Belo Horizonte, Brazil, in 1932. He earned licentiates in philosophy, literature, and theology from the Jesuit faculty in Nova Friburgo (Brazil), the Catholic University in Rio de Janeiro and the Jesuit faculty of Sankt Georgen in Frankfurt, Germany, respectively. He received a doctorate in sacred theology from the Gregorian University in Rome in 1968.

Libanio was a professor of theology in the department of theology at Catholic University, Rio de Janeiro, from 1972 to 1981. During this same period he was theological advisor to the National Conference of Religious in Rio de Janeiro. He was a member of the National Pastoral Institute of the Brazilian Bishops' Conference from 1971 to 1979. He served as Prefect of Studies at the Pontifical Brazilian College in Rome from 1963 to 1967; and was a member of John XXIII Jesuit Social Institute in Rio de Janeiro from 1975 to 1981. He presently serves as President of the Society for Theology and Sciences of Religion in Brazil; and since 1982 has been professor of theology at the Jesuit Center for Higher Studies in Belo Horizonte.

Living in Rome during and immediately after the Second Vatican Council, Libanio had first-hand contact with the winds of renewal sweeping through the Catholic church. This proved to be a major catalyst in his own theological growth and nurtured in him an increasing openness to the challenges of the modern world. Thus, by the time he returned to Brazil in the late 1960s, he was receptive to ecclesial and political renewal that was taking place in his own country. For the next decade he worked with high school and university students, encouraging their efforts to promote liberation in a country beset by repression and censorship. In the process Libanio was forced to sharpen his own critical awareness of the social and political problems that his country faced. Themes which were later to constitute an agenda for liberation theology, e.g. political conscientization of the poor, were already emerging in his work with these students. During this period he was introduced to the deception perpetrated by his own country's intelligence network when one of the supposedly most loyal members of his cadre of supporters turned out to be a military "plant."

Another significant factor in shaping Libanio's theology was his close friendship with Frei Betto and other Dominicans who had been jailed by the military regime for their political views. Since he and Frei were blood relatives, Libanio was allowed to visit his friend in the Presidio Tirandentes ("Toothpull" Military Prison) in São Paulo and, after Frei's release, to correspond and converse regularly with him. Libanio maintains that Frei strengthened and expanded his commitment to the liberation struggle. During the 1970s, Libanio's involvement in the National Pastoral Institute of the Brazilian Bishops' Conference brought him in contact with leading theologians and social scientists, notably Leonardo and Clodovis Boff, Carlos Mesters, and Pedro Ribeiro de Oliveira. These contacts, as he put it, further "fanned the flame of liberation" in him.

A final major factor in the development of Libanio's liberation theology has been his intimate involvement in many Christian base communities in Brazil since the mid-1970s. He has lived for long periods of time in many of the poorest regions in the interior of Brazil, working and talking and praying with base community personnel, pastoral ministers, religious, priests and bishops involved with these communities. He has participated in the Inter-Church Conferences of these base communities. His exposure to the intimate connection between faith and life, the gospel and political struggles among the poor, has been the primary catalyst for his theology of liberation.

Libanio's version of liberation theology has several dimensions. He is interested in an in-depth investigation of the connections between faith and politics, a theme that he develops in *Spiritual Discernment and Politics: Guidelines for Religious Communities*. Like so many liberation theologians he insists that the spiritual and political components of life must be closely intertwined. In his spiritual pilgrimage Libanio has shown a great appreciation for the writings of St. Ignatius on spirituality, especially Ignatius's emphasis upon the communal or corporate dimension of spirituality. Libanio also stresses the importance of the relationship between liberation theology and the ongoing Catholic tradition. He has made a thorough study of recent encyclicals that focus on social issues and points out how these documents have a direct bearing on the theme of liberation. Libanio believes it important not to treat liberation theology as a recent isolated phenomenon, but rather as a renewed emphasis on a vital segment of Catholic tradition. From this historical perspective an authentic theology must then discern the "signs of the times."

From the perspective of liberation theology, these signs are the situations of oppression and poverty that characterize Latin America. The most important task facing liberation theology today, Libanio believes, is "to undertake from a point of departure in a carefully analysed empirical basis, a sociopolitical elaboration of the data of revelation, with a view to a new understanding both of reality and revelation."

Marxism has influenced Libanio's thinking on social issues in two important ways. First, it has helped him identify those alienating forms of religion that do indeed perform as opiates in keeping the poor in an oppressed state. Here Marxism can assist in awakening Christians to the need for social transformation. Second, Marxism has helped Libanio see the need for the development of a political theology grounded in the existing politico-social situation. But for Libanio, Marxism's usefulness is strictly limited to social analysis; as a full-fledged ideology it has no value for the Christian faith.

Libanio's liberation theology, then, springs directly from an experience of God in confrontation with the poor; it is not a product of any political ideology. Libanio encourages serious and sympathetic dialogue between Christians and Marxists. Before the Nicaraguan Revolution, which gave power to the Sandinistas, and before Fidel Castro's recent religious overtures, Marxism as a phenomenon of political history seemed closed to any penetration on the part of Christianity. But today—whether because of a greater openness on the part of theology to social problems or because of the Christian collaboration with the Sandinista revolution—Christians and Marxists are more receptive to dialogue.

Libanio faults some critics of liberation theology for their failure to recognize its specifically theological dimension, considering it a mere sociology of liberation. He also objects to perceptions of liberation theology as an extension of the theology of violence and revolution. Libanio hopes his future writings will help to eliminate many of the misunderstandings concerning liberation theology by emphasizing the ways faith and politics, spirituality and social involvement, must always go hand in hand.

BOOKS

Spiritual Discernment and Politics: Guidelines for Religious Communities. Maryknoll, N.Y. : Orbis Books, 1982.

Fé e Política: Autonomias especificas e articulações mútuas. São Paulo, Brazil: Loyola, 1985.

ARTICLES

"Experiences with the Base Ecclesial Communities in Brazil," *Missiology* 8, 1980, pp. 319-338.

"Critérios de Autenticidade do Catolicismo," *Revista Ecclesiástica Brasileira* 36, 1976, pp. 53-84.

OTTO MADURO

Since 1965, I have been troubled by the existence of certain Latin American societies in which the majority of human beings are subjected to a harsh regimen organized to fatten the bank accounts of local and foreign minorities. This troubles me to the point of incapacitating me for any understanding or living of my gospel faith except by involvement in the struggle against this social regimen, which I perceive as unjust and transformable. And it troubles me to the point where I cannot submissively cross my arms in the face of certain allegedly "Christian" attitudes and traditions that appear to me to be an antievangelical instrumentalization of the church in the service of social injustice (Religion and Social Conflicts, p. 146).

Otto Maduro's principal contribution to liberation theology has been as a sociologist of religion who is critical of many of his colleagues in the field of sociology, who claim to be impartial in their scholarly critiques. He maintains that sociologists should be aware of their "inescapable partiality," while at the same time showing a willingness to criticize their own partial perspectives.

Otto Maduro was born in Caracas, Venezuela, in 1945. Both his parents were lawyers working with the government in family law. Both were politically involved in seeking social democratic change on behalf of the poor. Although his mother was nominally Catholic, Maduro's father was a professed atheist who would have nothing to do with the church. However, in 1960, influenced largely by a young Galician woman servant to his parents—"the first adult person I trusted and who trusted me"—Otto Maduro was baptized a Catholic. He joined a number of Catholic youth movements and in high school joined the Christian Democratic Party. Subsequently he joined anti-communist, armed clandestine Catholic brigades until 1963, when he entered a Roman Catholic seminary, albeit for only a few months.

Maduro entered the University of Venezuela in Caracas in 1964, and received a licentiate in philosophy in 1968. Up to 1966 he continued to participate in the Catholic anti-communist struggle taking place in Venezuela, although he himself had reached the point where he renounced the use of arms. During this period of his life, he contracted hepatitis and, while he was bed-ridden for several months, he took the opportunity to read the writings of such left wing Catholic radicals as Julio Silva Solar, Jacques Chonchol, and Camilo Torres; and for the first time he was introduced to the writings of Karl Marx. Much to his surprise, he found himself agreeing with Marx's social critique, and he concluded that in many respects Christianity in its basic social teachings was in fact closer to Marx than the Catholic church would officially acknowledge.

During his years as a student at the University of Venezuela, Maduro studied philosophy under liberal atheist professors; he worked among the urban poor and participated in the creation and subsequent activities of the Christian Left. From 1969 on, he became increasingly alienated from the Catholic church. Subsequently he studied at Louvain, receiving an M.A. in philosophy, a Ph.D. in 1977, and an M.A. in sociology of religion in 1978. He served as professor at the University of the Andes in Merida, Venezuela, from 1968 to 1985, and has taught at the University of Venezuela in Caracas and at Notre Dame University. In 1987 he began a three-year teaching appointment at Maryknoll School of Theology in New York.

During his years at Louvain, Maduro intensified his study of Karl Marx. Although he never became an avowed Marxist, he resonated with much of what Marx had to say about religion. He claims that Marx helped him see the "liberating potential" of the social teachings of Jesus Christ. While in Brussels, Maduro came under the influence of Gustavo Gutiérrez. He credits Gutiérrez with playing a pivotal role in his spiritual pilgrimage back to the Catholic church in 1976. Also influential in this regard were his contacts with the Christians for Socialism movement and the editorial staff of the magazine *La Lettre*. After a period of six years in Europe, Maduro returned to Latin America where he gradually identified himself with liberation theology as it emerged among the Christian base communities.

Otto Maduro has become one of the leading intellectuals in Latin American liberation theology. Three features of his version of liberation theology deserve special attention. The first involves his role as a sociologist who seeks to develop a sociology of knowledge in a Latin American context. His book, *Religion and Social Conflicts*, has this particular goal in mind. Maduro, as has been suggested, strongly criticizes his sociologist colleagues who claim to be impartial. Neutrality in social analysis, he insists, is not an option. Social analysis cannot escape philosophical and even theological implications. One cannot do sociology in a social vacuum. Further, as a sociologist Maduro believes that liberation theology must expand its vision beyond economic and political dimensions and give attention to four other issues that have strong social implications: the oppression of women; the struggle for world peace and the avoidance of nuclear war; the preservation of the natural environment; and the willingness to create the conditions for a pleasurable and sensuous life that radiates joy. This fourth item might come as a surprise. But why should theology be a grim enterprise? Without the sensuous ingredient, liberation is simply not complete—at least not "as we dream of it in the Caribbean."

A second feature is Maduro's critique of Marxism as an ideology. Maduro's views on Marxism have evolved through the years. In his early years, Marx was for him an arch enemy. Later he became sympathetic to Marxism as a means of understanding class struggle and capitalist exploitation, and how traditional religion has often functioned as the opiate of the masses. But in later years Maduro has become much more critical of both Marxist theory and practice. He is willing to accept some of the implications of Marxist social analysis without the ideological framework. He now talks of the need for the "desacralization of Marxism." By the use of this phrase he suggests: "Marxism is experienced by its new 'users' not as demanding a total allegiance, not as necessarily tied to certain parties and policies, not as requiring renouncement to religious conceptions and organizations, not as 'one, only and exclusive', but, rather, it is experienced as a disintegrated chaotic mass of 'tools' or 'instruments'—part of which might be appropriated, part of which may be rejected without any regret whatsoever" ("The Desacralization of Marxism within Latin American Liberation Theology," p. 8).

A third significant feature is Maduro's conviction that the Christian base communities in Latin America are both the harbinger of the future Catholic presence in that region and the repositories of the very best in Catholic tradition. These communities represent "the liberating sense of the unity, sanctity, catholicity, apostolicity and visibility of the Roman Catholic Church in Latin America." These small groups of Christians should not be seen entirely as innovations, but, rather, as extensions of the early Christian communities—in this way: These communities of poor and oppressed Christians seek to deepen their sense of oneness with all Christians. They acknowledge the sacred character of their wholistic liberating mission. They are catholic in their desire to develop the universal presence of the church as an open community struggling for the full realization of our best human potential as children of God. They are apostolic in their missionary expression of the good news of the Gospel. And they incarnate the visible church as they celebrate their calling as equal children of the same God. In displaying these marks of the church, which have come down from the first Christian era, these communities are a model in showing all Christians a new—yet old!—way of doing mission, one that is liberating and humble, open and caring, personal and communal, and includes the dimension of joy. Maduro maintains that "missioners as well as the oppressed themselves must nourish the capacity to enjoy, celebrate, increase and share life. This is a vital part of mission conceived as good news for the oppressed" ("Notes for a South-North Dialogue in Mission from a Latin American Perspective," p. 71).

BOOKS

Revelación y Revolución. Merida, Venezuela: Universidad de Los Andes, 1970.

Marxismo y Religión. Caracas, Venezuela: Monte Avila Editores, 1977.

La cuestion religiosa en el Engels premarxista. Caracas, Venezuela: Monte Avila Editores, 1981.

Religion and Social Conflicts. Maryknoll, N.Y.: Orbis Books, 1982.

Somos Negros. with Nancy Noguera. Caracas: Ediciones Ekare Banco del Libro, 1989.

ARTICLES

"Marxist Analysis and the Sociology of Religion: An Introduction," *Social Compass* (Belgium), 22, 1975, pp. 3-4.

"New Marxist Approaches to the Relative Autonomy of Religion," *Sociological Analysis* (Chicago), 38 (4), 1977, pp. 359-367.

"Labour and Religion According to Karl Marx," *Concilium*, 1980, pp. 12-20.

"Notes for a South-North Dialogue in Mission from a Latin American Perspective," *Missiology*, Vol. 15, No. 2, April 1987, pp. 61-77.

"The Desacralization of Marxism within Latin American Liberation Theology," address at the annual meeting of the Association for the Sociology of Religion, Chicago, August 13-16, 1987.

"The Liberating Sense of the Unity, Sanctity, Catholicity, Apostolicity and Visibility of the Roman Catholic Church in Latin America," unpublished paper.

JOSÉ PORFIRIO MIRANDA

The notion of communism is in the New Testament, right down to the letter (Communism in the Bible, p. 1).

169

José Porfirio Miranda is a professing communist for reasons he finds at the core of the New Testament: "All who believed were together and had all things in common; and they sold their possessions and goods and distributed them to all, as any had need" (Acts 2:44-45). Miranda faults other Latin American liberation theologians for their timidity in refusing to proclaim communism as *the* New Testament point of view, and he attributes their reticence to a fear of reprisal from the Catholic church. The end result is that the basic message of liberation theology has become blurred and equivocal.

José Miranda was born in Monterrey, Nuevo Leon, Mexico, in 1924. He did his graduate work in Europe, earning a licentiate in theology from the University of Frankfurt am Main, and a licentiate in biblical sciences from the Biblical Institute in Rome in 1967. He also studied economic theory at the universities of Münster and Munich. His broad academic training has led to his teaching mathematics, economics, philosophy, law, and the Bible at various institutions of higher learning in his native country, including the Instituto de Ciencias and Instituto Tecnologico in Guadalajara, the Instituto Regional in Chihuaha, and at both the National University and the Instituto Libre de Filosofia in Mexico City. Since 1974 he has been a professor at the Universidad Metropolitan Tztapalapa in Mexico City.

José Miranda has been advisor to student groups throughout his professional life. His activities in this capacity have often made him *persona non grata* to state authorities as well as the Catholic church. (He was once a Jesuit priest.) He has been expelled from three Mexican cities for his involvement in proletarian movements. But he has made his mark primarily as an academician who, as a result of his biblical and economic studies, has developed an avowedly communist stance. Miranda traces his conversion to communism to the early and middle 1960s. He recalls that when he "first grasped that the true God, the God of the Bible, can be known and approached only *through* the needy neighbor, my life changed entirely. Such a grasp was not an instantaneous event, it required some years, much reading, much meditation, especially much biblical study."

Miranda has concerned himself with giving Third World liberation theology a solid intellectual framework for advocating a communist point of view. Without rigorous biblical exegesis, he insists, liberation will only remain "a whimsical fad, a seasonal mode, an optional point of view among other optional points of view." But today's Christianity, he argues, does not need just one more option. If liberation theology is simply one alternative among many, then the oppressors' version of Christianity becomes as acceptable as the revolutionary version of Christianity. If that is the case, then one might just as well hold on to the traditional theology and ecclesiology of the church. What difference does it make? Miranda insists that today's proclamation of the Christian faith needs a forthright unambiguous decision in favor of the historical Jesus, what he actually taught and did; and the only means for achieving this goal is rigorous exegetical work that refuses to compromise.

During the mid-1960s, Miranda came to reject the Catholic church and all compromising maneuvers that try to mediate between church fidelity and fidelity to Jesus. He makes a crucial distinction between the Catholic church and what he considers to be the authentic teachings of Jesus. He maintains that if liberation theologians refuse to stand resolutely against the anti-liberation position of the Catholic church, then in a decade or two liberation theology will be compromised. It will, in effect, be nullfied by being absorbed into the Catholic church, a fate common to many revoutionary movements.

Although José Miranda has often been linked with the teachings of Karl Marx, he makes it clear that he is a communist and not a Marxist. In fact, he did not even begin to study the writings of Karl Marx and his followers until the early 1970s, nearly a decade after his conversion to communism. And even then his primary reason for studying Marxism was to find out what Marx and his supporters actually taught. Here again we note Miranda's basic concern to study systematically and critically the subject itself—whether it be the New Testament or Marxism—and not simply to accept automatically what others have said about the subject. So Miranda insists that Karl Marx and Marxist thought have had no significant role in the development of his own theological and biblical positions. In *Apelo a la Razon* (1983), Miranda contends that Marxism is based on a false thesis, namely, that the mode of production (i.e., the material world) determines the ideas of human beings. But he does argue that Marx himself is much better than subsequent Marxism, just as he believes that Jesus is far better than what the Catholic church has made of him. In one of his major books, *Marx against the Marxists*, Miranda makes the claims that "Marx felt an affinity to authentic Christianity: to the radical personality and message of Jesus Christ" (p. 225); and that both Marx and Engels believed that their understanding of communism was "a conscious continuation of authentic Christianity" (p. 240).

José Miranda, then, should be labeled a communist and not a Marxist, a point he expands upon in his *Communism in the Bible*. By communism he means holding everything in common and making distribution according to each one's need (Acts 2:44-45). He maintains that Jesus himself was a communist in that he advocated collective ownership. Based upon his exegesis of Scripture, he concludes, "the endorsement of communism—and above all of its reason for being, which is the intrinsic immorality of relative wealth and profit—is right in the Bible. And it is in the Bible in a fashion so unconcealable and cutting that the only logical thing for the establishment to do would be to shelve the Bible among the books of antiquities and cease to consider it a sacred book of normative character" (p. 57). "For Jesus there can be no social differences; Jesus' kingdom is a classless society" (p. 20).

But for Miranda, collective ownership is not the same as government ownership. State ownership does not substantially change capitalism, since only a minority of people continue to make the decisions about the use of the material resources. Miranda believes that the very definition of communism—collective ownership—implies complete democracy. Ownership by all the people means the obligation for everyone to participate in the decision-making process. Every member of the community should have a voice in how the resources of a given society should be distributed. A collective decision is impossible without a democracy. For this very reason Miranda believes that since the Russian and Chinese systems are not democratic, they are not really communistic.

In conclusion, José Miranda believes that a liberation theology that espouses the authentic teachings of Jesus is not a Latin American phenomenon. It has a universal character. At stake is the very purpose of Christianity: the establishment of a worldwide community of collective ownership in which the resources of the earth are distributed according to need. This, Miranda concludes, would be a world community fully in accordance with what Jesus actually taught.

BOOKS

Marx and the Bible. Maryknoll, N.Y.: Orbis Books, 1974.
Being and the Messiah. Maryknoll, N.Y.: Orbis Books, 1977.
Marx against the Marxists. Maryknoll, N.Y.: Orbis Books, 1980.
Communism in the Bible. Maryknoll, N.Y.: Orbis Books, 1982.

PABLO RICHARD

The church of the poor arises and develops in the heart of Christendom: hence we should not separate this new model from its "mother" institution prematurely. Little by little, however, it is becoming clear that the church of the poor is the only meaningful alternative for the future of the church. Perhaps old forms of Christendom will continue to exist long into the future. Nonetheless, I believe that the church of the poor will continue to gain ground as a credible and meaningful church, particularly in the eyes of the poor and the young" (Death of Christendoms, Birth of the Church, p. 191).

Pablo Richard believes that since the early 1960s there has been a growing structural crisis in the Catholic church—particularly in Latin America—a crisis in which the old established close working relationship between church and state, with the state as mediator, is breaking up. In its place there is emerging, from within Christian base communities, a new model of the church in which the poor and exploited become the agents of liberation. Richard sees as one of his major contributions to liberation theology the articulation of this new way of doing evangelization, pastoral activity, and theology.

Pablo Richard was born in Chile in 1939. From his earliest years he has been exposed to the reality of the extensive poverty throughout Latin America. "It has been the poor, the popular movement, the revolutionary processes, that have exerted the greatest influence on my life and my theology." After studying philosophy in Chile from 1957 to 1959, Richard traveled to Europe for his graduate work. He continued to study philosophy in Austria and then returned to his native country, where he received a licentiate in theology from the faculty of theology, Universidad Católica in Santiago in 1966. He was ordained a priest a year later. He returned to Europe to earn a licentiate in exegesis from the Pontificio Instituto Biblico (Rome) in 1969. He continued his studies in Bible and archeology at the Ecole Biblique in Jerusalem and received a Ph.D. in sociology from the Sorbonne in 1978. Richard served as Professor of New Testament, Faculty of Theology, Universidad Católica in Santiago from 1970 to 1973. Since 1978 he has lived in Costa Rica as a member of the Departamento Ecuménico de Investigaciones (DEI) as well as Professor of Theology at the National University of Heredia, Ecumenical School of Sciences of Religion.

Richard cites several experiences as "special moments" in his life story that have had a direct bearing on his theological development. During his years of teaching in Santiago, 1970 to 1973, he served as a pastor in a barrio where 120,000 people lived in extreme poverty. When Augusto Pinochet came to power through a military coup in 1973, Richard witnessed the persecution, torture, and in many cases, the death of his militant friends who opposed Pinochet's dictatorship. Richard himself fled from Chile as a political refugee and lived in exile in Paris for the next five years. These were troublesome years for him. He questioned the role of the Catholic church in Chile, and its cooperation with Pinochet and, as a result, he gave up his priestly activities. While he lived in Paris he married, and he now has three children.

In 1978 he moved to Costa Rica to take up his professorial duties. There he spent a considerable amount of time visiting and working with Christian base communities throughout Latin America. Over the next decade he became interested in the Sandinista popular revolution in Nicaragua. He made several trips to Cuba where he met Fidel Castro, a man who, Richard believes, is "one of the most exceptional persons of our century. He has brought me to an understanding of the world of the poor."

Richard cites several other individuals as having a decisive influence on his life, among them Bishop Pedro Casaldaliga and colleagues Gustavo Gutiérrez, Leonardo Boff, and Jon Sobrino. Perhaps the most important influence on the future direction of his life was the late Archbishop Oscar Romero of El Salvador. Richard believes that the poor Salvadoran people helped him "discover anew the presence and revelation of God in history, as the liberator God of the poor." And he goes on to say that "Archbishop Oscar Arnulfo Romero gave me my definite direction in my new life. Today I am exercising the priestly ministry again in the base communities in various countries of Central America."

Richard has concentrated much of his attention on the theological articulation of the new model of the church emerging from the Christian base communities. This model is built on a strong spiritual and biblical foundation. Richard strongly believes that "In spirituality is the root and strength of the theology of liberation." Liberation theology must never be wrongly perceived as a political ideology. Such a notion is patently false. "The object of liberation theology has *always* been *the God of the poor.*"

Richard readily admits that Marxist analysis has helped him to "understand reality, to de-ideologize theology, to overcome an idealistic view of the world. Of great utility to me has been the Marxist critique of religion, which only develops the biblical critique of religion and idolatry." Richard encourages dialogue with Marxists, many of whom he numbers among his close friends. He makes the point that the church should not be "anti-Marxist," but should be "non-Marxist." He goes on to explain that the church "does not make a class or socialist political option *as church.* It consciously keeps its distance from any kind of politicization, whether, theoretical, practical, or organizational, within the popular movement. This church, as a church, does not employ any political analysis of class and class struggle" (*Death of Christendoms, Birth of the Church*, p. 174). Richard insists that it is not Marxism, but the poor people, who have opened his eyes to a new vision of the church in the world. "The people of the poor themselves, organized and aware, have taught me, in everything, a new understanding of history and a new ethics. The people have a profound wisdom, acquired in centuries of struggle with domination. My principal university has been the popular movement."

Richard points out that in recent years the theology of liberation has taken on a more universal dimension. It now stresses the importance of liberation from sexism and cultural imperialism. Richard's own consciousness has been raised in journeys to New Delhi and Hong Kong. He has discovered that Latin America is but one part of the Third World and that the church of the entire Third World needs to be "decolonialized," that is, freed from its First World control and biases. This decolonialization of both theology and the church has become an important goal for Richard. As he expresses it: "Today the axis of the world runs from Pretoria to São Paulo to Santiago to Managua to New Delhi—not from New York to Paris to Moscow to Tokyo."

BOOKS

Cristianos por el Socialismo. Historia y Documentación. Salamanca, 1976.

La Iglesia latinomericcana entre el temor y la esperanza. Costa Rica, 1980.

The Idols of Death and the God of Life: A Theology. Pablo Richard et. al. Maryknoll, N.Y.: Orbis Books, 1983.

La Fuerza Espiritual de la Iglesia de los Pobres. Prólogo de Leonardo Boff. Costa Rica, 1987.

Death of Christendoms, Birth of the Church: Historical Analysis and Theological Interpretation of the Church in Latin America. Maryknoll, N.Y.: Orbis Books, 1987.

JUAN LUIS SEGUNDO

For me the greatest danger for faith continues to be the divorce between faith and life with its commitments (to use a formula of Vatican II). But I would like to carry this to a conclusion that, it seems to me, was not present in the Council and which, at least in our Latin American situation, I find absolutely decisive: I believe the dangers for faith are viewed in ecclesiastical circles as dangers that threaten orthodoxy. And they are viewed thus because it is supposed that faith is something that, on a par with the sacraments, has a kind of ex opere operato effectiveness for salvation. That is, that exactitude in the maintenance of dogma has an ex opere operato efficacy, which means that it is, up to a certain point, like a church possession, as if the church owned the truth....I believe that this is the greatest danger: to think that faith is a kind of possession of the church that is best preserved when the formulas are repeated in a strictly orthodox way and when the Christian stays away from dialogue with others who do not keep the faith in the same orthodox way. For me this is a vital concern: we are suffering because of it (Faith: Conversations with Contemporary Theologians, *p. 173*).

To keep faith and life, the supernatural and the natural, church and world together is perhaps the most important theme in the liberation theology espoused by Juan Luis Segundo.

Segundo was born in Montevideo, Uruguay, in 1925 and has spent most of his life in his native country. He studied theology in San Miguel, Argentina, in the early 1950s, and then matriculated to Louvain. He was ordained a Jesuit priest in 1955 and received a licentiate in theology from Louvain the following year. In 1963 the University of Paris awarded him a doctorate in philosophy and theology; Segundo specialized in ecclesiology and the writings of Nikolay Berdyayev.

During his years at Louvain, Segundo enrolled in a course on the theology of grace taught by Leopold Malevez. He recalls: "On the intellectual and theological level, what I have always understood as my own 'theology of liberation' began with him—a theology I amplified once I had returned to Latin America" (*Theology and the Church*, p. 75). Basically Malevez's contention was that faith must always be understood in its specific historical context, that God's grace is always implicit within human nature, in "pagans" as well as in believers. One, therefore, must never compartmentalize the sacred and the secular into two separate realms. Malevez traced this view to the Second Council of Orange in A.D. 529 and its espousal of the supernatural character of human faith. Segundo recalls how only a decade after Malevez had taught him that grace is a universal human condition, the church encyclical *Lumen Gentium* (Dogmatic Constitution on the Church) affirmed the same conviction, namely, that following one's conscience and seeking the good and the true in the human realm is an important prelude for receiving the gospel. Thus, Segundo argues that the seeds of liberation theology are to be found in Vatican II, so that by the time he returned to Uruguay in the mid-1960s he was already stressing the importance of maintaining a balanced perspective, which emphasized both God's grace and human initiative, that faith and life in their historical context are the cradle of God's salvific action.

When he returned to his native country, Segundo took a leading role in founding the Peter Faber Center in Montevideo, serving as its Director from 1965 to 1971. This center specialized in the sociology of religion and provided an important base for Segundo in developing his theology of liberation for Latin America. During the late 1960s, Segundo met with other Latin American theologians whose theological concerns converged with his own. He recalls one such meeting in particular, which took place in Petrópolis, Brazil, under the leadership of Ivan Illich. Here Segundo and his life-long friend, Gustavo Gutiérrez, presented position papers which Segundo claims constituted the framework for the emerging theology of liberation. This small cadre of theologians continued meeting over the next several years and proved to be an important catalyst for both Segundo and Gutiérrez for their theological growth.

The Peter Faber Center also gave Segundo the opportunity to forge his theology of liberation. In collaboration with his colleagues there, between 1968 and 1972, Segundo produced a five-volume work entitled *A Theology for Artisans of a New Humanity*, which was a course in theology specifically for lay people and had as its starting-point the everyday lives of these lay people. Topics covered in these volumes include the church, grace and the human condition, ideas of God, the sacraments, evolution, and guilt. Here we see the spirit of Vatican II and the importance that Segundo attaches to the intimate connection between the divine and the human. The church is a creative minority, a community of believers who know "the mystery of love "(Vol. I, p. 55). Grace is "the new life brought by Christ "(Vol. II, p. 9). When we "dedicate our effort and our lives to the work of fostering mutual respect and love and unity" among all persons, we are one with God, "whether we are aware of it or not" (Vol. III, p. 57). The sacraments are community gestures that associate us "with the perennial questions of humanity" (Vol. IV, p. 74). Interestingly, Segundo himself has never taught as a university professor in his native country (although he has held visiting professorships in the United States), but has concentrated his attention on the everyday lives of the poor. He continues to serve as a chaplain to various lay communities throughout Uruguay, his major vocation since the late 1960s.

Over the years, Juan Luis Segundo has been a prolific writer. Although one cannot do justice to the richness and diversity of his writings, three additional features of his theology of liberation will be singled out here. The first is his intention to develop a methodology appropriate for the Latin American setting. His book, *The Liberation of Theology*, based on a series of lectures he gave at Harvard, is his major effort in this regard. Here he follows up his basic contention that theology must emerge from the historical condition of the powerless, and he affirms a methodology for doing this which he calls the "hermeneutic circle," which in essence stresses the need for a continuing dialogue between the Bible and present-day historical realities. "The circular nature of this interpretation stems from the fact that each new reality obliges us to interpret the word of God afresh, to change reality accordingly, and then to go back and reinterpret the word of God again, and so on "(p. 8). Segundo examines the views of several leading First World contemporary theologians, contending that theological methodology must be liberated from captivity to the rich, the powerful, and the academics.

A second feature is Segundo's major undertaking to date: his concern to articulate a full-blown theology of liberation for Latin America today, a five-volume effort under the general title, *Jesus of Nazareth, Yesterday and Today*. In volume one, *Faith and Ideologies*, Segundo continues to develop his basic theme that faith and life are inextricably related, showing that the radically social character of faith necessitates keeping faith and ideology in juxtaposition. There can be no such thing as pure faith devoid of particular ideological interests. He contends: "A faith without ideologies is a dead faith, a faithlessness. If an absolute is unwilling to immerse itself in the relative, it ceases to be absolute....It is inferior to 'live' ideology" (p. 129). In volume two, *The Historical Jesus of the Synoptics*, Segundo focuses on Jesus' parables, with the intention to "talk about Jesus in such a way that it may open up people to seeing him as a witness to a more humane and liberated life " (p. 16). Here Segundo maintains that Jesus was an ordinary lay person who held no special clerical title, a fact which, Segundo says, makes Jesus so utterly real to lay people. He is one of them! In volume three, *The Humanist Christology of Paul*, Segundo concentrates on the first eight chapters of Paul's letter to the Romans to show the political implications of Paul's views for today. Paul can open up for us a "humanizing political realm that no repression can control or render useless" (p. 10). The apostle Paul "personifies *the forces that intervene significantly in every human life*, the forces that any human being will detect when it looks into the depth of its own existence, regardless of outer circumstances or religious background" (p. 10). In volume four, *The Christ of the Ignatian Exercises*, Segundo shows the direct relevance of the christology of the *Spiritual Exercises* of Ignatius of Loyola for today.

One final feature that deserves attention is Segundo's continuing involvement in the contemporary debates taking place within the Catholic church. Consider, for example, the controversy over capitalism versus Marxism-socialism. Segundo believes it important to utilize the insights of Marxist analysis. But this does not make him a Marxist any more than utilizing some of the ideas of Aristotle makes him an Aristotelian." ...the great thinkers of history do not replace each other; rather, they complement and enrich each other. Philosophic thought would never be the same after Aristotle as it was before him. In that sense all Westerners who philosophize now are Aristotelians. After Marx, our way of conceiving and posing the problems of society will never be the same again...In that sense Latin American theology is certainly Marxist. I know my remark will be taken out of context, but one cannot go on trying to forestall every partisan or stupid misunderstanding forever" (*The Liberation of Theology*, p. 35).

One other example. In 1984 the Vatican's Congregation for the Doctrine of the Faith under the leadership of Cardinal Joseph Ratzinger issued a document, "Instruction on Certain Aspects of the 'Theology of Liberation,'" which criticized some elements of Latin American liberation theology. Segundo has responded to this document with his book, *Theology and the Church*, contending that it is, in essence, a negative evaluation of the contributions of Vatican II. Segundo asserts: "Let me be clear: I understand that my theology (that is, my interpretation of Christian faith) is false if the theology of the document is true—or if it is the only true one" (p. 14).

To keep faith and life together is the cornerstone of Segundo's theology of liberation. To underscore this point, Segundo concludes his book, *Theology and the Church*, by quoting Cardinal Henri de Lubac: "If I lack love and justice, I separate myself completely from you, God, and my adoration is nothing more than idolatry. To believe in you, I must believe in love and justice, and to believe in these things is worth a thousand times more than saying your Name" (p. 156).

BOOKS

Faith: Conversations with Contemporary Theologians. Edited by Teofilo Cabestero. Maryknoll, N.Y.: Orbis Books, 1980.

The Hidden Motives of Pastoral Action: Latin American Reflections. Maryknoll, N.Y.: Orbi Books, 1978.

A Theology for Artisans of a New Humanity. Volumes 1 to 5. *The Community Called Church, Grace and the Human Condition, Our Idea of God,*

The Sacraments Today, Evolution and Guilt. Maryknoll, N.Y.: Orbis, 1973-1974.

The Liberation of Theology. Maryknoll, N.Y.: Orbis Books, 1976.

Theology and the Church: A Response to Cardinal Ratzinger and a Warning to the Whole Church. Minneapolis: Winston Press, 1985.

Jesus of Nazareth, Yesterday and Today. Volumes 1 to 5. *Faith and Ideologies, The Historical Jesus of the Synoptics, The Humanist Christology of Paul, The Christ of the Ignatian Exercises, The Evolutionary Approach to Jesus of Nazareth.* Maryknoll, N.Y.: Orbis Books, 1984-1988.

ARTICLES

"The Church: A New Direction in Latin America," *Catholic Mind,* March 1967, pp. 43-47.

"Christianity and Violence in Latin America," *Christianity and Crisis,* March 4, 1968, pp. 31-34.

"Social Justice and Revolution," *America,* April 27, 1968, pp. 574-577.

"Has Latin America a Choice?" *America,* February 22, 1969, pp. 213-216.

"Wealth and Poverty as Obstacles to Development," *Human Rights and the Liberation of Man.* Edited by Louis M. Colonnese. South Bend, Indiana: University of Notre Dame Press, 1970, pp. 23-31.

"Capitalism-Socialism: A Theological Crux," *Concilium 96: The Mystical and Political Dimensions of the Christian Faith.* Edited by Claude Geffre and Gustavo Gutiérrez. New York: Herder and Herder, 1974, pp. 105-127.

"Statement," *Theology in the Americas.* Edited by Sergio Torres and John Eagleson. Maryknoll, N.Y.: Orbis Books, 1976, pp. 280-284.

JON SOBRINO

It can be historically verified that the various interpretations of liberation theology in Latin America seem to agree on one point: If a Christology disregards the historical Jesus, it turns into an abstract Christology that is historically alienating and open to manipulation. What typifies Jesus as a historical reality is the fact that he is situated and personally involved in a situation that displays structural similarities to that of present-day Latin America. At least we can detect a similar yearning for liberation and a similar situation of deep-rooted sinfulness. It is the historical Jesus who brings out clearly and unmistakably the need for achieving liberation, the meaning of liberation, and the way to attain it (Christology at the Crossroads, p. 353).

Jon Sobrino is perhaps best known for his articulation of a christology geared to the Latin American setting, a setting that he believes parallels the historical situation in which Jesus lived.

Jon Sobrino was born in Barcelona, Spain. Growing up in a
Basque family during the Spanish Civil War, he came to know at
an early age the ravages of war and the sufferings of the poor and
oppressed, an experience that later became influential in the development of his theology of liberation. He received his master's
degree in mechanical engineering at St. Louis University in 1965
and then decided to study theology and become a priest. Ordained
a Jesuit priest, he received his doctorate in theology from the
Hochsuchle Sankt Georgen in Frankfurt in 1975. He is now professor of philosophy and theology at the Universidad José Siméon
Cañas of El Salvador.

Jon Sobrino is a firm believer in the dogmas of the Catholic
church as interpreted by the church's magesterium. He acknowledges "the irreplaceable role of the christological dogmas of the
church for liberation theology" (*Jesus in Latin America*, p. 19), and
insists that "there is no reduction of the total truth about Jesus
Christ in the christology of liberation, either in intent or in fact"
(p. 53). An authentic Christology, he believes, can be developed
only "within the framework of the trinitarian reality of God"
(*Christology at the Crossroads*, p. xxiv).

Having made clear his Catholic orthodoxy, however, Sobrino
insists that the New Testament contains many different christologies and that each of these christologies can be understood and ap-
preciated only within its own particular historical setting. Sobrino concludes from this that an adequate christology for Latin
America must emerge from the Latin American setting of poverty
and oppression. One must not, therefore, superimpose a christology
on Latin America "from above." The New Testament is first an
historical document and second a theological proclamation that
emerges from the historical. Sobrino writes: "Looking for an objective starting point means looking for that aspect of the total and
totalizing reality of Christ that will enable us to find access to
the total Christ. Here I propose the historical Jesus as our starting
point. By that I mean the person, proclamation, activity, attitudes, and death by crucifixion of Jesus of Nazareth insofar as all
of this can be gathered from the New Testament texts....This particular starting point contrasts sharply with any christological
approach that *begins* its reflection with the already glorified

Christ" (*Christology at the Crossroads*, pp. 351-352). Any christology that ignores its historical basis, Sobrino insists, remains
abstract and open to manipulation.

What is the historical situation of Latin America today? It is
the irruption of the poor and dispossessed in seeking liberation
from the bonds of servitude. Sobrino asserts: "The most fundamental datum in this connection is the fact that life is being threa-
tened and annihilated by structural injustice and institutionalized
violence" ("The Witness of the Church in Latin America," p. 164).
It is at this point—the historical condition of the poor and oppressed in Latin America—that the person of Jesus comes alive
and takes on flesh and blood. Here, Sobrino declares, we have
"the figure of a Jesus of the poor, who defends their cause and
takes up their lot, who enters the world's conflict and dies at the
hand of the mighty, and who thus proclaims and is good news
that is still fundamentally and eternally new" (*Jesus in Latin
America*, p. xv). Latin American liberation theology, Sobrino concludes, must be profoundly christological.

As noted earlier, Sobrino sees many similarities between the
Latin American historical context and the times in which Jesus
lived. This is an important point for Sobrino. He writes: "...there
is a clearly noticeable resemblance between the situation here in
Latin America and that in which Jesus lived...the resemblance
does not lie solely in the objective conditions of poverty and exploitation that characterize Jesus' situation and ours, as well as
many others throughout history. It lies primarily in the cogni-
zance that is taken of the situation....The whole complex of
themes that surrounds the historical Jesus coincides greatly with
that which now surrounds Latin America" (*Christology at the
Crossroads*, pp. 12-13). Jon Sobrino faults other Latin American
theologians for not giving sufficient attention to the development
of a full-fledged christology for Latin America. (Leonardo Boff is
an important exception.) This may in part be the reason why Sobrino devotes so much attention to this theme. He returns to it
again and again in his writings. Only Jesus can offer the poor and
dispossessd the fullness of life. The lack of this fullness, Sobrino
asserts, "is not caused only by the limitations of what has been
created, but rather by the free will of minority groups, who use
their power for their own interests, and against others. That is
why Jesus anathematizes the rich, the Pharisees, the scribes, the
priests, and the rulers: because they deprive the majorities of life,

in its various forms" ("The Epiphany of the God of Life in Jesus of Nazareth," p. 76).

Another important component to Sobrino's theology of liberation is the concept of the kingdom of God. We learn about the historical Jesus in the context of the reign of God. Sobrino points out that Jesus "did not preach about himself, or even simply about God, but rather about the kingdom of God" (*Christology at the Crossroads*, p. 60). To affirm the kingdom of God is to affirm a reign of justice and liberation. The kingdom of God, Sobrino declares, "will be that situation in which human beings have genuine knowledge of God and establish right and justice toward the poor" (*Jesus in Latin America*, pp. 88-89). In God's kingdom the poor are the favorites. It is precisely for this reason that Jesus directed his preaching at the plight of the poor. Sobrino goes on to say: "The absolute for Jesus is what he *maintained in deed* as ultimate through his life, throughout his history and in spite of history: the service and love of the oppressed, in order to create a world in which right and justice will be established—a world worthy of the undying hope that, despite all, the kingdom of God is still at hand" (p. 94).

Sobrino makes no use of Karl Marx or Marxist analysis. When he does refer to Marxism, it is usually in the context of his discussions of the views of European theologians like Pannenberg and Moltmann. Like most other Third World liberation theologians, Sobrino finds in his Christian faith the motivation for his condemnation of the glaring political, socio-economic inequalities so pervasive in Latin America today. The terms *socialism* and *capitalism* are not to be found in the indexes of his books.

In short, Jon Sobrino is an orthodox Roman Catholic whose experience of living with the poor in Latin America has given him a new vision of the meaning and significance of Jesus Christ for the poor. This figure of Jesus ministering to the poor in Latin America is the key to his theology of liberation. It is for this reason, Sobrino confesses, that "I keep writing and publishing about Jesus, occasionally making theoretical advances and occasionally 'repeating the same thing.' " (p. xv).

BOOKS

Christology at the Crossroads: A Latin American Approach. Maryknoll, N.Y.: Orbis Books, 1978.

The True Church and the Poor. Maryknoll, N.Y.: Orbis Books, 1984.

Theology of Christian Solidarity. With Juan Hernandez Pico. Maryknoll, N.Y.: Orbis Books, 1985.

Jesus in Latin America. Maryknoll, N.Y.: Orbis Books, 1987.

Spirituality of Liberation. Maryknoll, N.Y.: Orbis Books, 1988.

ARTICLES

"The Witness of the Church in Latin America," *The Challenge of Basic Christian Communities*. Edited by Sergio Torres and John Eagleson. Maryknoll, N.Y.: Orbis Books, 1981, pp. 161-189.

"The Epiphany of the God of Life in Jesus of Nazareth," *The Idols of Death and the God of Life*. Edited by Pablo Richard *et al.* Maryknoll, N.Y.: Orbis Books, 1983, pp. 66-103.

ELSA TAMEZ

*The story told in the various biblical accounts is one of op-
pression and struggle, as is the history of our Latin American people. In fact, our present story can be seen as a continuation of what we are told in biblical revelation. For this
reason, I think that reflection on oppression and liberation
in the Scriptures is not to be regarded simply as a study of
one more biblical theme. Rather oppression and liberation
are the very substance of the entire historical context
within which divine revelation unfolds, and only by reference to this central fact can we understand the meaning
of faith, grace, love, peace, sin, and salvation (Bible of
the Oppressed, p. 1).*

Elsa Tamez has made her contribution to Third World liberation theology primarily in two significant areas. First, she has
taken the biblical theme of oppression/liberation—which she
notes is almost entirely missing from the writings of First World
theologians—and has applied it to her own Latin American context. Second, she has begun to focus more specifically on sexist oppression, believing that women liberation theologians have a special responsibility to make explicit how the biblical theme of
oppression/liberation is related to their every day life struggles.

Elsa Tamez was born in Victoria City, Tamaulipas, Mexico in
1950, but she grew up in Monterrey, Nuevo Leon. Her family, which
consisted of eight brothers and sisters, was very poor, so she knew
firsthand the stark reality of poverty and suffering. Tamez credits
both her mother and her local Presbyterian church for providing
the foundation for her continuing strong biblical faith. When she
was fifteen years old she moved with her family to Mexico City to
seek better living conditions. Three years later, Tamez went to Costa Rica to live. Her growing religious convictions led her to enroll
in the Latin American Biblical Seminary in Costa Rica, from
which she received a master's degree in theology in 1979. Since
that year she has taught biblical studies at the Seminario Biblico
Latinomerica in San Jose and is also on the staff of the Departamento Ecuménico de Investigaciones (DEI). In the meantime, she
has continued with her formal education, earning a master's degree in literature and linguistics in 1985 from the National University in San José. In 1987 she took a leave of absence from her teaching responsibilities to move to Lausanne, Switzerland, to complete
work on her Ph.D. Her doctoral dissertation focuses on a Latin
American rereading of the doctrine of justification by faith. She
has been active in the Methodist church of Costa Rica—there is no
Presbyterian church in her area—and has regularly taught a Sunday School class for adults in which she has sought to relate biblical teachings directly to the lives of her students.

Tamez traces her predisposition to liberation theology back to
her years in Monterrey and her own personal struggles against poverty in the midst of the revolutionary turmoil of Central America.
Here once again she points to the strong religious faith of her
mother and her church—"I always felt that God was a close friend
of mine"—with providing the basis for her growing conviction
that poverty and oppression are contrary to God's will. Later she
was exposed to liberation theology at the Latin American Biblical

Seminary and especially at the DEI (of which Hugo Assmann was the founder and director), and this forced her to rethink the direct relevance of biblical teaching to her own historical setting, where life and death are constantly struggling with one another.

To date, Tamez's major book in English is *Bible of the Oppressed*. Here she makes a careful study of the theme of oppression/liberation and how this theme sheds light on Central America. The oppressors, both as told in the Bible and as witnessed in Central America, are primarily the wealthy, the ones in political power, whose main ambition is to increase their wealth at the expense of the poor. The powerful control the destiny of the oppressed. They are the idolators who distort the teachings of the one true God because "they need other gods who will lend justification to their own sinful deeds" (p. 34). Yet the poor know that God is not indifferent to their plight, for God is a liberating God who sides with them. "The message of the Good News is of the liberation of human beings from everything and everyone that keeps them enslaved. That is why the Good News brings joy and hope" (p. 68).

In a later book, *Against Machismo*, Tamez zeroes in on sexist oppression. This book consists of a series of interviews with leading male Latin American liberation theologians in order to find out their own views concerning sexist oppression. She concludes: "If Latin American men do not recognize the reality of women's oppression, if they do not admit that they are promoters or accomplices of the ideology of machismo that permeates our culture, if they do not realize how great the riches that are lost to society due to the marginalization of women, if they do not move from theoretical conviction to liberating practice, if they do not join in solidarity with women in their struggle, the path of the feminist movement in Latin America will be longer, the progress slower and often more bitter, with more frustration than joys" (p. vii).

In her focus on sexist oppression, Tamez shows the importance of a fresh interpretation of many of the biblical stories. For example, in her article "The Woman Who Complicated the History of Salvation," she retells the story of Abraham and Sarah. In the usual telling of this story the emphasis is on Sarah as God's chosen one. God's favor is shown in Sarah's giving birth to Isaac at an elderly age. But what about Hagar, the lowly Egyptian concubine who earlier had borne Abraham's child Ishmael? Why do we pass over her when we speak of God's favorites? Hagar and her son,

Ishmael, are the "marginalized in history" who never make the headlines, who are banished to the desert because of Sarah's intense jealousy. But note in this story how Hagar retains her dignity despite Sarah's action. Hagar refuses to be humiliated. It is God who opens her eyes and gives her and her son the courage to struggle against discrimination and hardship. Ishmael—which in Hebrew means "God hears"—will be free, because God has heard his cries of injustice. "Hagar and her son will be free from Egyptian oppressors and Hebrew discrimination. They will be one with Yahweh, the Lord...for God will always be ready to help those in search of a new life. The poor complicate the history of salvation. But God's action on their behalf teaches us that we should reconstruct this well-known history" (p. 39). And if God hears the cries of the biblical Hagar and Ishmael, what about the Hagars and Ishmaels of Central America?

The lack of Marxist influence in Tamez's analysis of the causes of oppression can be noted in her comment: "Marxism is a discipline that I must study in these next years. I recognize its great importance and my lack of greater knowledge." She sees the obvious importance of class analysis in understanding poverty and oppression in Central America, but finds that category too limiting. What about racism? Tamez herself is of mixed race. What about sexism? Not only the working classes of people, but also natives, blacks and women of all classes must become the subjects of liberation theology if it is to be all-encompassing.

As a woman of mixed race, Elsa Tamez, in her own personal life struggles, is well aware of the complexities attached to the theme of oppression/liberation. Her concentration on a re-reading of the Bible in the context of this general theme, with a special emphasis on sexism and racism; her close involvement in the life of the church—which she sadly notes has for the most part ignored the realities of oppression—and her own unyielding conviction that God "comes on the scene as one who favors the poor" (*Bible of the Oppressed*, p. 72), have combined to give Elsa Tamez a special role among Third World liberation theologians.

BOOKS

La Hora de la Vida, 1978.

Bible of the Oppressed. Maryknoll, N.Y.: Orbis Books, 1982.

Against Machismo. Oak Park, Illinois: Meyer-Stone Books, 1987.

ARTICLES

"The Woman Who Complicated the History of Salvation," *Cross Currents*, 36, Summer 1986, pp. 129-139.

"La fuerza del des Nudo," *El rostro feminino de la teologia*, San Jose: DEI, 1986.